LETTERS AGAINST
THE FIRMAMENT

Sean Bonney

LETTERS AGAINST
THE FIRMAMENT

ENITHARMON PRESS

First published in 2015
by Enitharmon Press

www.enitharmon.co.uk

Distributed in the UK by
Central Books
99 Wallis Road
London E9 5LN

Distributed in the USA and Canada
by Independent Publishers Group
814 North Franklin Street
Chicago, IL 60610
USA
www.ipgbook .com

ISBN: 978-1-910392-15-7

Enitharmon Press gratefully acknowledges the financial support of
Arts Council England, through Grants for the Arts.

Individuals continue to sustain the Press through the
Enitharmon Friends Scheme. We are deeply grateful to all Friends,
particularly our Patrons: Colin Beer, Duncan Forbes, Sean O'Connor
and those who wish to remain anonymous.

British Library Cataloguing-in-Publication Data.
A catalogue record for this book is available
from the British Library.

Designed in Albertina by Libanus Press
and printed in England by
Short Run Press

CONTENTS

THREE LETTERS: AUGUST 2011

Anyway, I've totally changed my method. A while ago I started wondering about the possibility of a poetry that only the enemy could understand. We both know what that means. But then, it might have been when I was walking around Piccadilly looking at the fires, that night in March, my view on that changed. The poetic moans of this century have been, for the most part, a banal patina of snobbery, vanity and sophistry: we're in need of a new prosody and while I'm pretty sure a simple riot doesn't qualify, your refusal Set to leave the seminar room definitely doesn't. But then again, you are right to worry that I'm making a fetish of the riot form. 'Non-violence is key to my moral views', you say. 'I am proud of the fact that I never invented weapons to kill', you say. But what about that night when we electrocuted a number of dogs. Remember that? By both direct and alternating current? To prove the latter was safer? We'd taken a lot of MDMA that night, and for once we could admit we were neither kind, nor merciful, nor loving. But I'm getting off the point. The main problem with a riot is that all too easily it flips into a kind of negative intensity, that in the very act of breaking out of our commodity form we become more profoundly frozen within it. Externally at least we become the price of glass, or a pig's overtime. But then again, I can only say that because there haven't been any damn riots. Seriously, if we're not setting fire to cars we're nowhere. Think about this. The city gets hotter and deeper as the pressure soars. Electrons get squeezed out of atoms to produce a substance never seen on Earth. Under such extreme conditions, hydrogen behaves like liquid metal, conducting electricity as well as heat. If none of that happens, it's a waste of time. Perhaps you think that doesn't apply to you. What inexhaustible reserves we possess of darkness, ignorance and savagery. A hundred million people use electricity and still believe in the magic power of signs and exorcisms, in the nightmare of their lives as slaves to the rich. Don't pretend you know better. Remember, a poetry that only the enemy can understand. That's always assuming that we do, as they say, understand. Could we really arrive at a knowledge of poetry by studying the saliva of dogs? The metallic hydrogen sea is tens of thousands of miles deep.

August 5th 2011

We're beginning to suffer here. Obviously I've not been getting much writing done. But I've been thinking about the conversation we had, the last time we met. You remember, about Milton? Christ. Yours was such an obvious bourgeois response. Pandemonium is suburbia, pure and simple. The rioters are speaking in perfect English. It's the middle-class, the magistrates, and you, who are all talking some weird, ignorant slang. All of your mouths are stitched up with some kind of weird gaffer tape. Your laboratory is a slum. Sorry. I don't mean to be rude, but things have been pretty stressful. You know how it is when you read an account of a situation you've been directly involved in, but each one of its constituent parts has been extracted, polished, entirely rearranged? Last week was exactly like that. I got home and tried to phone you, but all that came out the receiver was a complicated, monstrous hiss. I did my best to explain it and came up with this, let me know what you think. Was it (a) you were speaking in a strange new language that had no place in my part of town, or (b) you were speaking at a specific frequency that only particular dogs could hear or use, or was it (c) the static that's left after the tape containing all your reason and superstition runs out and everything's revealed as it really is for one beautiful moment, all brightly lit in shopping mall reds and flickering striplight yellow. I've been wearing a black balaclava for days. From what I can tell, your part of town has been taken over by a weird parade of quacks, magistrates and fortune tellers, all yelping as if everything that happened over the past week was the result of a possession by some kind of evil spirit, and they could only ward it off with a display of archaic gestures, vicious combinations of letters and numbers. The magistrates have taken on the condition of people, and the people round here are no longer to be honoured with even a human shape. It's a curious process. We see it everywhere: in the movements of musical notes, of chemistry, steam and water, of birth and death. Each syllable is a different tonal cluster, penned in with police-wire and used electricity. I hear you're thinking about becoming a bailiff. In any case, I'm glad they burnt your laboratory down. Now send me some fucking money.

August 20th 2011

It's difficult to talk about poems in these circumstances. London is a razor, an inflamed calm has settled, we're trapped outside on its rim. I've been working on an essay about Amiri Baraka, trying to explain the idea that if you turn the surrealist image – defined by Aimé Césaire as a 'means of reaching the infinite' – if you turn that inside out what you will find is that phrase from Baraka: 'the magic words are up against the wall motherfucker'. It's going very slowly – hard to concentrate what with all the police raids, the punishment beatings, the retaliatory fires. It'd be too much to say the city's geometry has changed, but it's getting into some fairly wild buckling. It's gained in dimension, certain things are impossible to recognise, others are all too clear. I wish I knew more about maths, or algebra, so I could explain to you exactly what I mean. So instead of that I'll give you a small thesis on the nature of rhythm – (1) They had banged his head on the floor and they were giving him punches. (2) He was already handcuffed and he was restrained when I saw him. (3) He was shouting, 'Help me, help me'. (4) He wasn't coherent. (5) I went to speak to his mum. (6) He couldn't even stand up after they hit him with the batons. (7) They knocked on her door three hours later and told her 'your son's died'. I can't remember exactly where I read that. I'm pretty sure it wasn't in a literary magazine, but I guess you'll have to agree it outlines a fairly conventional metrical system. Poetry transforms itself dialectically into the voice of the crowd – René Ménil made that claim way back in 1944 or something. But what if that's not true. What if all it can do is transform into the endless whacks of police clubs – certainly you get that in official poetry, be it Kenny Goldsmith or, well, anyone. Their conformist yelps go further than that, actually, as the police whacks in their turn transform into the dense hideous silence we're living inside right now, causing immediate closing of the eyes, difficulty breathing, runny nose and coughing. Because believe me, police violence is the content of all officially sanctioned art. How could it be otherwise, buried as it is so deeply within the gate systems of our culture. Larry Neal once described riots as the process of grabbing hold of, taking control of, our collective history. Earlier this week, I started thinking that our version of that, our history, had been taken captive and was being held right in the centre of the city as a force of negative gravity keeping us out, and keeping their systems in place. Obviously I was wrong. It's not our history they've got stashed there – it's a bullet, pure and simple, as in the actual content of the collective idea we have to live beneath. They've got that idea lodged in the centre of Mark Duggan's face – or Dale Burns, or Jacob Michael, or Philip Hulmes. Hundred of invisible faces. And those faces have all exploded. Etcetera. Anyway, this is the last letter you'll be getting from me, I know you've rented a room right at the centre of those official bullets. It's why you have to spend so much time gazing into your mirror, talking endlessly about prosody. There is no prosody, there is only a scraped wound – we live inside it like fossilised, vivisected mice. Turned inside out, tormented beyond recognition. So difficult to think about poems right now. I'm out of here. Our stab-wounds were not self inflicted.

August 30th, 2011

LAMENTATIONS

for Jacob Bard-Rosenberg

Our illnesses are mostly political illnesses
PETER WEISS

We greet the dark
DIANE DIPRIMA

in the days of our fiercest anger

the precision of beauty
the joy   of the whole world

soaked bread   in their darkness
enemies pressed their mouths on us

a snare is come among us
there are none to comfort us

Of music imprisoned, the insulted and truly wretched.
Of the names of those responsible for the recent massacres.

On the numerology of birdsong
On riot replaced by birdsong
Our persecutors swifter than eagles

They pursued us on the mountains. Laid wait for us in the wilderness.

And our collective vowels humming like drones.
The invisible, whatever that is.
As if it didn't hover above us.
Announce itself with blue fire.

The law is a mouth.
Glossolalia.

these towers and cities
these desert plains
these tasteful burning
skies, what are they
what has been forgotten
in these shanty towns
these parks and legends
solid, bright, concealed
strange and distant
ghosts, our stark ghosts

pass the soul of your body like water
boiling water that scalds forever

It breathes, the law, and those it protects it sings inside, and they
are like flowers, chaste and tranquil as glass.

It stares at us, the music of the law, and its fingers, they pluck us, as
if we were strings, golden, and we are their songs, the inhabitants
of the law.

And we have no foothold, and we stumble, backward and back-
ward, hour by hour, as stars or buildings collapsing, into the abyss,
of their hearts, the inheritors of the law, and we sing there, unimag-
ined, in the ice of our silence, falling.

And their souls will flow like piss in the streets of the great city.

Say they have enclosed us in blank stone. You wake up, you open your eyes, is simple: we have been consumed like blood and water, and our language – you wake up, sibilants and syntax a jet of bleach and concepts. Think stuff up: the enemy is non-material, we are not.

Say they have choked us with black sugar. Ask who are these custodians of yesterday's rebellions – insist that it really happened, we are not at all imaginary. You wake up, you open your eyes – there is a border separates us, the deserving, the un-deserving dead. Post no miracles.

this is you

It is the stupid practice of our times to complain instead of acting. Jeremiads are the fashion. Jeremiah is found in all attitudes. He cries, he lashes, he dogmatises, he dictates, he rages, himself the scourge of all scourges. Let us leave the elegising clowns, those gravediggers of liberty. The ~~duty of a revolutionary is to always struggle, to struggle no matter what, to struggle to extinction.~~

lol das you bro

LOUIS-AUGUSTE BLANQUI.

five days without sleep
the law is fixed and burns
we who are captive here
each night the same figure
on the same road, stops
roaring, like a brain
roaring out our ghosts
hyacinth and snap-flower
my ghosts, a river of bones
my ghosts, narcissi my
spinning, my laws, stay here
'evil-doing falls like rain'

remember it
to take these tales as advice
an organising vortex
       each sentence stolen
each word a double claw. Act now.

That looked the sun in the face and were not blinded

LOLA RIDGE

So anyway, insomniacs or the wandering dead sleep by walking
through the department, yeh, through the golden city. Well screw
them. The choir, if there is one, is a flock of ghosts. The chorus a
mob of disenchanted sloganeers. Forget it. Take some sulphate,
some hydrogen, whatever, elements, elementals, mash it all up
and *boil* the invisible

       the ecstasy of oxygen molecules
       the mad monks of Westminster

       One was scried with swallows.
       One was split with scissors.

       some grow in dust
       are not to be picked
       opponents of day
       and night's
       counter-light

every door is not locked

ERICKA HUGGINS

Because we do not exist the years of our birth are stacked inside the shadows of our mouths like imaginary cities or the pits of heaven and other basic banalities.

And when they say 'we', they are only trying with their drivel to mould what the people think and how they think it.

ULRIKE MEINHOFF

'We' the liars. 'We' the obedient, 'we' the imperial teeth.
No birds, no suits, no sacrificial spiders.
This history passes through us like ghosts.
Various acronyms. Nostalgia for electric colour.
Black and murderous pink.

Say those rats. Say those rats have names say you know those names. You do not know those names. Say black powder say a lot of things. And then, a fascist victory, say that. And then. Say it seemed like a door was opened like just for a second and we hurtled through that door or was it things hurtled toward us I don't know and. Say it was just a cloud of powdered blood. Say you know their names and then suffer from beneath those names and live and tunnel inside those names and. Ask what becomes of the motherfucking broken hearted

Avoid melancholy.
Tell a few jokes.
Blow up Stonehenge. NO

apply gravity to your body
raw water like butter actually
made from your body, yes, meaning
you, we, 'a force from the past'
& on the subject of flowers:

Who are these judges, who made them custodians? Of what?
What are these things in the centre of their mouths, that ringed
silence, that crushed clock, screams of dead and flying things. The
human form, it frightens me, its scratched and monstrous aspects;
plague clung to, as spirit of love, and spectres shriek like starlings
in the streets of our devastated cities.

it is a storm of monstrous drums

the war has not been declared
                    it only shrieks
the way ghosts shriek &
        ashes are the shrieks
                    of ghosts are
burnt water   are skalds
of coins & lawful slumber

and scarlet stars of rotten silver

I want to never forget how I was forced to become a monster
of justice and intolerance, a narrow minded simplifier, an
arctic character uninterested in anyone who was not in league
with him to kill the dogs of hell

RENÉ CHAR

21

there is a law it
patrols the invisible
is dark outside

there are comets as
we decipher them
as law or radio

as then the cities burn
as ash as simple figures
as the sky is an insult

name this city

it is a bone it is
our bones creak
as pearl fire will

split nets of streets
or bone it is
no emergency

& this sentence
　　　un-pronounced
must not make you bitter
　　it has made you bitter

– it is our beauty, apocalyptica –

But for you it would be something of a duty in that you could
perform in Tübingen the role of a waker of the dead. It is true that
the Tübingen gravediggers would do their utmost against you.

HÖLDERLIN to HEGEL, 25 November 1795

CORPUS HERMETICUM:
ON THE REVOLUTIONS OF
THE HEAVENLY SPHERES

News blackouts etc. This really happened.

Every Thursday mayhem in weather systems.
Imaginary battles in science and strike actions. The bastards had
    won
as in Vision overload, fascist analysis of human beings
and a slightly less comfortable suburb. Arts and that.
Or science. Black mirrors. Seven dials. Black mirrors. Seven dials.
    Prisons.

We're blocking central London. Riot as, in relation to this past
I don't need a wound. We wanted going fucking mad. Too many
    racists still breathing
and strange convulsions, I felt it, me and the devil
at first repression and counter-acts, overload Malediction, tried to
    chart strikes
as Noise, they were still dead. Their galaxies, spinning faster.

Mercury unsuitable for making coins.

February 17th 1600, burned, 'his tongue imprisoned because of his
wicked words'

for water say plague i.e. the language of judges, the infinite vowel
for water say fire i.e pulsars and mace. For water say yellow fire
i.e. the fascist microbe in every drop of rain. For water say dust
i.e. negative flames, soluble dust, chemical burns, scars and skies

Forget psychogeography. All it's ever been is a ring of protection, a
police-thing's joy, at its centre that bitter knot of strings that Brecht
called 'prophecy', spy-rings. String One: we were smashing up the
Ritz, March 2011. String Two: shit was talked about immigrants,
about dole scroungers. String Three: not an ATM a bright metallic
wind or real-time alignment of the patterns of non-affordable

housing scattered throughout the city and the stereo-optic beat-
ing of police hearts. Beat one. Cancellation of Europe and Mercury.
Stone circles are police kettles, you can't tell me different.

for yellow fire say fuck the police
kill fear say fire say fuck the police

For example, take Newgate. Built 1188, directly into the walls,
London's eastern gate. Beat Two. We don't recognise ourselves
there. Beat Three. The debtor's jail, the throat the muzzle of the
city. July 10th, 1790, burned. Robert Peel built cops from the
ashes. Beat Four. Debt is bone. Versions of bone. Version One.
Spare change. Version Two. Lock the bosses out. Superglue them.
Out. Version Three. Debt One. Those nobility who entered the
city from the east would pass through a wall packed with the
tortured, the scraped and wheezing dead. London a cursèd city,
is beautiful in the smouldering spring.

> We're not underground we're invisible.
>
> BERNARDINE DOHRN

remember Theresa May, that guillotine
Unemployed families were slaughtered
remember Theresa May driving thru London in crackling human
    Tar
about legal channels, hot pink and petrol flare
Awake at night, in strike actions

or the protests did what in relation to Fucking realism
stuck it out inside all noise, inside David Willetts and Abiezer
    Coppe
bounded by law, David Willetts, gored by magpies and glass
Victory to dole scroungers. This really happened

inside Normal matter such as atoms and electrons, orphanhood.

Check the extent of police lines. 1829, Robert Peel invented 1000 pigs to circle the city as walls or gates as cordons. This happened. Those 1000 pigs as calendar, the working day a pyramid as razor the police recuperation of the sun. It was dark and the barricades were burning.

Tiresias the birds. Tiresias who sees what only a child could see, who blunders up from hell and hell is not underground. Says riots are a work of vast and incomprehensible mourning, a border a burning weird as even the fear felt by Charles and Camilla, that crow-bait, 2010, off with their heads – this really happened we have no fucking demands and Tiresias summoned voices of the vast dead charts of incomprehensible bird flight, everywhere we are those birds and it don't mean shit the cops don't know this.

> We're not all white and we're not all men
>   – George Jackson Brigade Communiqué, 1976

Robert Peel still peers down from Broadgate wall and is a blockade, Newgate torched. Police moved in smashed heads in counter-time, a silent musical fixture separates a human being from a cop. It is vital to recognise, to insist on that difference, that fixture – to locate with precision where that separation first appears in the 'continuum' where the entire pack of errors, superstitions and blood-stained bullets ram the solar throat of every cop in this town with vile psychic music and we live there, have organised noise. Studied strikes. Cop lives don't matter.

> We must cry out in anguish now
> to know the wound
> to understand its nature and extent . . .
>   Anonymous Weather Underground poem, *circa* 1975

for 'I love you' say fuck the police, for
'the fires of heaven' say fuck the police, don't say
'recruitment' don't say 'trotsky' say fuck the police
for 'alarm clock' say fuck the police
                                    for 'my morning commute' for
'electoral system' for 'endless solar wind' say fuck the police
don't say 'I have lost understanding of my visions' don't say
'that much maligned human faculty' don't say
'suicided by society' say fuck the police, for 'the movement
of the heavenly spheres' say fuck the police, for
'the moon's bright globe' for 'the fairy mab' say
fuck the police, don't say 'direct debit' don't say 'join the party'
say 'you are sleeping for the boss' and then say fuck the police
don't say 'evening rush-hour' say fuck the police, don't say
'here are the steps I've taken to find work' say fuck the police
don't say 'tall skinny latté' say fuck the police, for
'the earth's gravitational pull' say fuck the police, for
'make it new' say fuck the police
                               don't say 'spare change'
say fuck the police, don't say 'happy new year' say fuck the police
perhaps say 'rewrite the calendar' but after that, immediately
after that say fuck the police, for 'philosopher's stone' for
'royal wedding' for 'the work of transmutation' for 'love
of beauty' say fuck the police
          say no justice no peace and then say fuck the police

LETTERS ON HARMONY

Somewhere in London there is a judge who, every seven days, pays a prostitute to re-enact the crimes of those he has sentenced that week, while he looks on and masturbates. Sorry, I've been trying and I just can't get that sentence right. I read about it this morning on Facebook and, you know, it's annoying, I was hoping to make some progress on the thoughts I've been developing on the Pythagorean system of harmonics, and how it relies on a consciously fictional central point in order to keep its symmetrical force stable. There's a passage on it in Lenin's Collected (Vol 38), and I think it might be helpful, tho for what I'm not quite sure. But anyway, I couldn't stop thinking about this judge. And then I started thinking, well, what if – and sure it's a pretty big if – but what if he was producing these emissions quite deliberately, as the source of a central vibration through which the judiciary could impose a new and extremely rigid analysis of the city, within which a sterile atmosphere could be maintained for the propagation of a limited number of official sentences (say, for example, seven) from which all possible thought could be derived. Sex magic, yeh. All of that ludicrous shit. Don't think I'm turning into one of those wankers in David Icke masks: in terms of creation myths it's a fairly traditional narrative structure. What this judge probably doesn't realise, however, is that each of his particle jets will necessarily invoke an adjunct sentence, which while in its weak form may only be manifest in certain cries of disbelief and fear, in extreme conditions may – and that's a very big 'may' – may ultimately manifest as a ring of antiprotons, otherwise known as attack dogs. Hackney, for example. These attack dogs are stable, but they are typically short-lived since any collision with an official sentence will cause both of them to be annihilated in a brief but highly intense burst of energy. In other words: buy a gun, learn to shoot it, get a rudimentary job in the high court, and then do some very simple equations. Hope you're well, by the way. The sky over London is milky and foul.

November 11, 2011

OK let's try again. Though bear in mind, this is gonna be naive as all hell. I mean, I haven't done the requisite study, of what harmony is and what it has been etc. What I can gather, from a careful reading of some of Lenin's Notes on Hegel – he's got something in there about the Pythagorean harmony of the spheres proposing a perfect cosmology, a hierarchy built on scalar realities that justifies social conditions on earth, where everybody is in their place, and nobody is able to question the beauty and perfection of these relationships. Straightforward. And for it to work, for all these justifications to hold true, a fictional body is essential: the antichthon, or counter-earth. Thus, at the limit, the gravitational pull that holds the entire system of hierarchical harmony together is an untruth, but an untruth with the power to kill. But if this untruth is the site of justification and corporate (i.e. ritual) slaughter it's also the site, magnetic as all hell, of contention and repulsion, which can transgress its own limits until something quite different, namely, crime, or impossibility, appears. For Ernst Bloch, the revolution was the crossroads where the dead come to meet. For Lorca, music was the scream of dead generations – the language of the dead. But our system of harmony knows so well it contains its own negation that it has mummified it, and while we know we live within a criminal harmony, we also know we are held helplessly within it as fixed subjects, or rather as objects, even cadavers, of an alien music. But never mind, just as protest is useless only because it stays within the limits of the already known, so the hidden harmony is better than the obvious. Heraclitus. Music as a slicing through of harmonic hierarchies etc, poetic realities as counter-earths where we can propose a new stance in which we can see and act on what had previously been kept invisible etc. Ourselves, for one thing. That sounds just great, absolutely tip fucking top, until you remember that, equally, the harmony of the money fetish is that of the commodity fetish only now become visible and dazzling to our eyes, i.e. we don't have any kind of monopoly on harmonic invisibility, and all of those occultist systems that some of us still love so much have always been bourgeois through and through. That is, it's not a question of gentrification, but that the whole process has always started from the invisible spot where your feet are, tapping whatever fetishised rhythms right into the star encrusted ground. That famous green door with its sign 'no admittance except on business'. That is, however much we may claim that it is not protest, but a fast alteration in the structural scansion at the city's core, the hidden contours of our songs are still a nasty little rich kid fluttering his hecatombic chromosomes all over our collective history. Shit. It's why I still hate *Mojo* magazine. OK. Now lets get really obvious. Once, revolutions took their poetry from the past, now they have to get it from the future. We all know that. Famous and so on. In its contemporary form, the slogan Greek anarchists were using a couple of winters ago: we are smashing up the present because we come from the future. I love that, but really, it's all just so much mysticism: but if we can turn it inside out, on its head etc we'll find this, for example: 'the repeated rhythmic figure, a screamed riff, pushed its insistence past music. It was hatred and frustration, secrecy and despair . . . . That stance spread like fire thru the cabarets and the joints of the black cities, so that the sound itself became a basis for thought, and the innovators searched for uglier modes'. That's Amiri Baraka, a short story called 'The Screamers' from 1965 or something like that. That is, metallic, musical screeches as systems of thought pushing away from, and through, the imposed limits of the conventional harmonic or social systems, thus clearing some ground from where we can offer counter-proposals. Slogans. The battle-cries of the dead. Tho, obviously, Pizza Express and the Poetry Café have done as much as is in their power to neutralise any truth content that might be lurking within that possibility. On September 30th 1965, Pharoah Sanders, McCoy Tyner, Donald Rafael Garrett, Jimmy Garrison, Elvin Jones and John Coltrane recorded the album *Live in Seattle*: it is, according to someone quoted on Wikipedia, 'not for those who prefer jazz as melodic background music'. It's one of those examples of recorded music that still sounds absolutely present years after the fact, because it

34

was one of the sonic receptacles of a revolutionary moment that was never realised: that is, it has become a Benjaminian monad, a cluster of still unused energies that still retain the chance of exploding into the present. Play it loud in the Walthamstow shopping mall and you'll see what I mean. Yeh yeh yeh. I'm thinking about a specific moment on the album, around thirteen minutes into 'Evolution', when someone – I don't think it's actually Coltrane – blows something through a horn that forces a dimensional time-loop through the already seismic constellations set up within the music's harmonic system, becoming a force that moves beyond any musical utterance, while still containing direct, clear communication at its centre: dialectical love, undeclared logic. Etc etc etc. I guess Seattle, like anywhere else, is sealed up in its gentrification by now. But anyway, that horn sounds like a metal bone, a place where the dead and future generations meet up and are all on blue, electric fire. CLR James once said that 'the violent conflicts of our age enable our practised vision to see into the very bones of previous revolutions more easily than before'. Go figure. Due to its position in the Pacific Ring of Fire, Seattle is in a major earthquake zone. On November 30th 1999 Seattle WTO protests included direct and rational attacks on, among other things, the Bank of America, Banana Republic, the Gap, Washington Mutual Bank, Starbucks, Planet Hollywood etc etc etc. 'Cosmos'. 'Out of this World'. 'Body and Soul', you get what I mean. Two years later, in Genoa, the anarchist Carlo Giuliani got a police bullet in the centre of his face. Remember that name. Capital's untruth, its site of corporate slaughter – i.e. ritual slaughter – the silent frequency at the centre of its oh so gentle melodies. Ah, I can't see to finish this, I've had a lot of valium today. But anyway, to put it simply, the purpose of song is not only to raise the living standards of the working class, but to prevent the ruling class from living in the way that they have been. The violent conflicts of our age make it impossible to recollect musical emotions in tranquillity, unless it is the kind of tranquillity that makes clear the fierce shrill turmoil of the revolutionary movement striving for clarity and influence. A high metallic wire etc. The counter-earth rigged to such sonic stroboscopics that we, however temporarily, become the irruption into present time of the screams of the bones of history, tearing into the mind of the listener, unambiguously determining a new stance toward reality, a new ground outside of official harmony, from which to act. Or put it another way, next time some jazz fan tells you that late Coltrane is unlistenable, or something, laugh in their ridiculous face. Seven times. More later.

December 16, 2011

I've been thinking about the riots again lately. It seems to me, sometimes, that the week in which they happened has been compressed, buried somewhere in the distant past, and we've all been trapped within its shell. Nothing has happened since then, nothing at all – or rather, everything that has happened has been blind scratchings at the walls of that week, on and on, hurtling further and further back in time. It's a purgatory which I suspect we will only be able to escape from when Margaret Thatcher dies. Can you understand what I'm saying? Actually, I was talking to a friend a couple of days ago about what 'understanding' might actually mean. 'Understanding', he said, 'is precisely what is in-compatible with the bourgeois mind'. For some reason I started thinking about the final scene in Lindsay Anderson's film *If*. You know it, of course – everybody does. Malcolm McDowell and his crew are sitting on the roof of the school, firing at all the teachers and parents and other kids, and then in a brief pause, the head-master steps forward. He thinks he's such a liberal, you recall. 'Boys', he implores. 'boys – I understand you'. Yeh. And so the character played by Christine Noonan – one of the few characters in the film who isn't a 'boy' – she shoots him right in the centre of his forehead. You know what I'm getting at – that bullet is his understanding, plain and simple, tho I'm not quite clear just how incompatible it is with the headmaster's presumably bourgeois sense of beauty, love and imagination, or indeed his understand-ing, ultimately, of himself and of everything else – including his killer. A killer who is identified only as 'the girl' in the cast list, even tho she's obviously the central figure in the film. Anyway, I'm getting off the point: Margaret Thatcher, and her strange relation-ship with the combined central nervous systems of all of the people who were picked up in the weeks following the riots, around 3000 of them. It is, of course, a very tricky equation, and has to take into consideration all of the highly complex inter-actions between the cosmological circuit of the entire history of the city (as perimeter) with the controlled circle of each of the riot prisoner's skulls (at the centre). There are those who say Thatcher is just a frail old woman and we shouldn't pick on her. I prefer to think of her as a temporal seizure whose magnetosphere may well be growing more unstable and unpredictable, and so demonstrably more cruel, but whose radio signature is by no means showing any signs of decreasing in intensity any time soon. They can hear it on fucking Saturn. The paradox being, of course, that Thatcher herself sits far outside any cluster of understanding the bourgeois mind could possibly take into account. But in any case, it's clear to me the heroes of Lindsay Anderson's *If*, had they lived, would have ended up as minor members of the Thatcher Cabinet, or at least as backbench Tory MPs. But we don't know whether or not they do live: the film freezes on McDowell, sliding down the school roof, blasting away, his face not quite fearful, not quite anything. Then silence. Just like the riots, they stay where they are, and so does everything else, fixed into that single, fearful second. According to some cosmological systems, and ones not so far removed from our own as we would maybe imagine, when anyone dies – be that Margaret Thatcher or Mark Duggan – they take their place among what are called the 'invisibles', traditionally opening up a gap in social time, a system of antimatter in which nobody can live, but from which new understandings and arrangements of social harmony may be imagined. Music, for example. Or the killing of a 'king', etc. But while I'd like that to be true, its essentially hymn-singing, a benevolent glister on the anticyclonic storms of business-as-usual rotating counterclockwise at ever increasing speeds into the past and into the future. I take those 'invisibles' as being not too dissimilar to so-called 'undesirables', all those refugees banged up in the various holding cells that cluster in rings outside airports and cities etc. That is, objects of human sacrifice which vicious and simplistic systems use to sustain a sinister and invisible harmony where everything spins on its own specified orbit and everything remains in its preordained place; everything that is except the ever increasing density of suffering, as pressure increases and one by one we vanish into some foul and unlikely parallel dimension. You know, like a government building or something. A cathedral, for example. Or a medieval jail. Or a Heckler & Koch MP5 (Police Issue). Anyway, I'm rambling now. I know full well that none of the above is likely to help us to understand, or break out of, or even enter, the intense surges of radio emissions we're trapped inside. Cyclones and anticyclones. Like, I'm certainly not proposing Thatcher as a counter-sacrifice, however tempting and, in the short term, satisfying that may be. It would be impossible: every *Daily Mail* reader would understand exactly what we were doing. It's horrible. I feel like it's gonna be the 6th August 2011 for ever. Christ, for all I know it's still 13th October 1925. The estimated costs of the August Riots were around £100 million. You can get 46 rounds of the ammunition that killed Mark Duggan for 15 dollars and 99 cents. On Amazon. For the police it's probably far cheaper, and right now that's the clearest definition of harmony I can get to. Happy new year.

January 31st, 2011

Sorry I've not written for so long, I've been pretty busy, and on top of that things have been getting rough again. I'm gonna have to go on the dole soon, and I'm really not looking forward to it. Don't get me wrong, I don't feel any guilt about it, not at all. The pittance they give us is an insult anyway. It's not even the workfare programmes, it's just that the Job Centre, the whole process, is a nightmare. Years ago they used to play music in those offices, I don't think they do anymore. It was always the same old predictable crap, yet played just below the standard audibility range. Yeh, I guess that's one way of thinking about the unshielded harmonic condition common to everyone with less than five pounds in their pocket. The weird gnosticism we live inside these days. The social truths that only those who live far below the hunger line have access to. Them, and of course the very rich. As if the rich were some kind of jagged knife, out on the social perimeter, and we, the very poor, were being scraped against that knife, over and over. All of you people in the middle – no matter how much you do care – are really just sleepwalking. It's why I get so incensed when you chastise me for the violence in my work. I mean, what do you dream about? My dreams are identical with those of several Tory MPs. Except, of course, I have them when I'm awake. But anyway, whatever, I don't mean to go on about my problems: I'm supposed to be writing to you about music, so let's just think about those songs they used to play in the Job Centre. All of the latest chart hits, converted into a high, circular whine, and in the centre of that whine an all too audible vocabulary. Money. Sanctions. Etc. That whine, that disaudibility, is fascinating. It's supposed to be. To be honest, I'm surprised it's not been taken up by The Wire. I'm surprised there aren't CDs, gigs in the Café Oto. I mean, it's a very interesting listening experience. You move in slow motion. You feel like you've just been injected with 300 mg of burning dog. Grammar and syntax can no longer be controlled. Speech, which usually would be your means of entry to actual lived time, is compressed and stretched into a network of circles and coils, at its perimeter a system of scraped, negative music, and at its centre a wall. And then you wake up after a night of terrible dreams to find you are that wall. See you soon, I hope. Isn't it about time you had me round for dinner?

April 5th, 2012

then we do admit we wish to do harm
its harmonic system of social chords
we are not that
a nasty little rich kid, his chromosome
all over my grandfather's memory
that receptacle of song
insulted and completely ruined

far into the night we spoke of death, of
white death was molten, reticent and black
was the tidy vortex at the city's core
its rim of cutting wheels
its theory of proletariat gravity
already knows exactly what you are
the perimeter scratches are fearsome

Thanks for your list of objections. I accept most of them: my vocabulary, my reference are for the most part things I've pulled from the past. Old films, old music. Old riots too, of course. All abstractions. It's exactly the same as going to the supermarket. The instore radio, the magazines, the DVDs, all of them register some kind of obsessive relationship with the culture's recent past, cut through with glints of austerity and empire. You know what my position on that is, but still, I quite like it in the supermarket. I go there every day, in fact I rarely go anywhere else. It's a kind of map of the future of London, adjusted to admit a slightly censored collective history, where friendly and antagonistic forces confront each other with rapidly diminishing strength. Astrology, basically. Or at least some form of stargazing. A weird constellation of information, fact and metaphor imprinted on the gridplan of the shop. It's a substitute for the calendar, basically, a system of harmony set up to keep us all, in a sense, intact. Some kind of corporate stability. It's why they only play certain songs in there. Simply Red, for example. I've got history with them, actually. You don't wanna know. Anyway, I was walking round there the other day wondering what it would be like if they played Leadbelly's 'The Gallis Pole' on their radio. I mean, obviously, nothing would happen. But, I dunno, let's pretend. It would be a laugh with the refrain, with 'did you bring me the silver, did you bring me the gold' going on and on and round and round. Gallows and ghosts and rings of flowers. It's a great song, the guitar picking sounds like a spiderweb. It's like a trap. Christ, it'd be awful. We wouldn't be able to get out, we'd be trapped inside and all light and sound in the place would be reduced to a frequency spectrum of predominantly zero power level: the forced unity of a few almost inaudible bands and spikes. Products, yeh, goods. All known popular songs would be seen flickering and burning like distant petrol towers in some imaginary desert, the phase velocity of the entire culture as a static sequence of rings, pianos, precious stones and prisons. Workfare: the explosion that lights up the abyss. Tempo, temperature, tempest. Temporary contracts. At no pay. Etc. Every song, including Leadbelly, underwrites that. But, and this is important, equally, the circulation of those songs does still contain within itself the possibility of interruptions. I was following the strikes at Walmart with great interest, for example. So were you, I guess. I mean, you're not some kind of idiot. Anyway, part of what those strikes communicated was, basically, this; the structure of the supermarket is kept in place, but all of a sudden the base astrological geometry of the place is revealed as simplistic, fanatic and rectilinear, stuffed with wounded human bodies that would prefer not to die. Repellent, preposterous, absolute monsters. The point is when all of that is no longer a metaphor. Like, for instance, time contracts in struggle, did you know that? The expansion the corporate hour needs in order to bleed us to scurvy, it snaps back, like some kind of medieval allignment of the planets. A sinister arithmetic suggesting that if they are not actually won, strikes will simply take their place among the racks of DVDs. Cracked one, absolutely unplayable, but there. You see what I mean? Subtract the vortices of supermarket consciousness and it's a cold and bitter landscape. Cold petrol, hydrogen ice. The circles of the sky as a rim of music, all vocabularies reduced to an entire symphony of separations. The deep truth is imageless. When you know that, you know there's everything to play for. All else is madness and suffering at the hands of the pigs.

October 14th, 2012

October 2012: Blanqui is still in jail, and as the cosmological city plan becomes ever more compressed, each human body comes to resemble a conspiratorial cell. This is individualism: all of us fixed into a collective table of anti-matter that no-one believes in, despite how much its wild flashing may sometimes portend trouble. Official speech takes on the rhythms of chicken bones, glue and feathers cast across a receding social sphere, and the antiphonic interplay of megaphones disperses like the dust of imploding stars. Within this reactionary net, the poem is negation, which simply means that it is false. A hopeless omen that longs to rupture the tyrannical banality of the 'true'.

I've been getting up early every morning, opening the curtains and going back to bed. There have been rumours of anti-unemployed hit squads going around, and I don't want some fucker with a payslip lobbing things through my window. Especially not when I'm asleep. Though I don't expect to be able to fool them for long – my recent research involves an intense study of certain individual notes played on Cecil Taylor's 1966 album *Unit Structures*, and so obviously, once I've managed to isolate them, I have to listen to these notes over and over again, at very high volume. Someone from the Jobcentre is bound to hear them eventually and then, even though I'm not claiming benefits, my number will, as they say, be up. Taylor seems to claim, in the poem printed on the back of the album, that each note contains within it the compressed data of specific historical trajectories, and that the combinations of notes form a kind of chain gang, a kind of musical analysis of bourgeois history as a network of cultural and economic unfreedom. Obviously, I've had to filter this idea through my own position: a stereotypical amalgam of unwork, sarcasm, hunger and a spiteful radius of pure fear. I guess that radius could be taken as the negation of each of Taylor's notes, but I'm not sure: it is, at least, representative of each of the perfectly circular hours I am expected to be able to sell so as to carry on being able to live. Labour power, yeh. All of that disgusting 19th-century horseshit. The type of shit that Taylor appears to be contesting with each note that he plays. As if each note could, magnetically, pull everything that any specific hour absolutely is not right into the centre of that hour, producing a kind of negative half-life where the time-zones selected by the Jobcentre as representative of the entirety of human life are damaged irrevocably. That's nothing to be celebrated, though. There's no reason to think that each work-hour will not expand infinitely, or equally, that it might close down permanently, with us inside it, carrying out some interminable task. What that task is could be anything, it doesn't matter, because the basic mechanism is always the same, and it involves injecting some kind of innovative emulsion into each of those hours transforming each one into a bright, exciting and endlessly identical disk of bituminous resin. Obviously, what is truly foul is what that resin actually contains, and what it consists of. It's complicated. The content of each hour is fixed, yeh, but at the same time absolutely evacuatated. Where does it go? Well, it materialises elsewhere, usually in the form of a set of right-wing gangsters who would try and sell those work-hours back to you in the form of, well, CDs, DVDs, food, etc. Every-thing, really, including the notes that Cecil Taylor plays. Locked up in cut-price CDs, or over-priced concert tickets for the Royal Festi-val Hall, each note he plays becomes a gated community which we are locked outside of, and the aforementioned right-wing gang-sters – no matter that they are incapable of understanding Taylor's music, and in any case are indifferent to it – are happily and oblivi-ously locked inside. Eating all of the food on the planet, which, obviously enough includes you and me. That is, every day we are eaten, bones and all, only to be re-formed in our sleep, and the next day the same process happens all over again. Prometheus, yeh? Hang on a minute, there's something happening on the street outside, I'm just gonna have to check what it is. One of those stupid parades that happens every six months or so, I imagine. One of those insipid celebrations of our absolute invisibility. Christ, I feel like I'm being crushed, like in one of those medieval woodcuts, or one of those fantastic B Movies they used to show on the TV late at night years ago. Parades. The undead. Chain gangs. BANG. 'Britain keeps plunging back in time as yet another plank of the welfare state is removed' BANG our bosses emerge from future time zones and occupy our bodies which have in any case long been mummi-fied into stock indices and spot values BANG rogue fucking plan-ets BANG I take the fact that Iain Duncan Smith continues to be alive as a personal insult, ok BANG every morning he is still alive BANG BANG BANG. I think I might be getting off the point. In any case, somewhere or other I read an interview with Cecil Taylor, and he said he didn't play notes, he played alphabets. That changes things. Fuck workfare.

November 24th, 2012

FROM *THE COMMONS*

SET ONE

the cuckoo is a pretty bird
she warbles as she flies

The cuckoo is a
BANG –
he was a big freak:
weirds have wrappt his
hail & gunnery,
his pronouns & his minds:
watching some documentary
scales, words stalked them,
warbled as they –
equated money with intelligence,
used the word 'reverie'
clean as a dipped saint –
I don't eat that bread /
yesterday I was still dead.

My character was taken
was not yours, who
secretly my small thighs
& the british anarchist movement
stayed indoors:
halt, magnetic sea
& shun mad company.
halt, intelligence
I got my goose shoes on
& talk eclipse, the town is stupid
love fool love,
or we could brick their windows
the aged parents broken,
exposed to annoyance & danger

Back when I was still cruel –
OK, say that again
this time with malevolent roses,
some specks of lords, some
totally harmless character:
the town's last cinema is broken,
& the rest were maimed & slain.
OK, say the word brain,
this time with malevolent roses
mumbled as in a 'reverie'
like lingerie & a clean blade
OK, do that again
we got from London what we needed
slaughter the fascist BNP.

O bitter magnet, we shine
inside the most vivid colours
– archaic pop reference here –
but my methods are scholarly
like many a gallant gentleman
I lay gasping on the ground
magnetic & flashing
as any wild-wood swine
we spoke with hail but
my methods –
'most fertile yuppie scum'
my methods are –
I seem to have anarchic tendencies
but I hang around with Trots.

O bitter mag –
what her lawyer called a brain snap
was a naked man, was cruel
after suffering: you can't have
your eyes / ran trickling
although she is your wedded
weird –
I bet he did I bet he
ran trickling down his knee, by fire
I bet he fell down those
warbled thighs –
you cannot have her eyes –
the final host of the murdered soul
net

obviously they read books in hell:
they are passionate and scared,
intersected at bitter angles /
the british anarchist movement,
its scales & documents
splintered under a false full moon
embroidered over with burning gold
not
we don't know who they are
not
intersected at oblique angles,
the power to hurt, for example
splat –
in London town where they did dwell.

Anyway, eclipse, as I was saying
with my small brain broken
inside the most vivid moments
with hail scales and etc –
yuppie characters –
slaughter the suffering moon
or watch some documentaries
flashing like zombies
or intelligence
inside our rumoured eyes –
oh pity / aged anarchists are scared
but obviously this reverie, intersected
the police system of knowledge
gargled with gold.

I bet she did I bet she
got up & performed his ambitions
my malevolent shine
gonna build me a log cabin
night of the living dead
jokes about gordon brown
something called the english democrats
on fire:
she would beat them to ashes
with a ring of teeth
& roses –
say cuckoo –
got up this morning
performed my alienations

Meanwhile, in the fast world of banking
they are thinking in blocks of sound
blank ones
reduced to little knots
of hair & teeth
we were speaking
like any gasping swine,
the still full moon
his character
splintered under a london town
that didn't become power:
I, trickling down her 'reverie'
of impending cash doom
& how to eat brains.

History is irrelevant with
ARCHAIC CREDIT REFERENCE HERE
the sun has been disconnected
& we, with our downturned mouths
are maidens,
our credit ratings threaded with flowers.
& we are bleating,
& we are fucking immense
shrieking with gibes & curses –
history, too, is a sort of zombie
secretly
swallowed by insatiate fiends
packed in every domestic second
forgetting to pay the bills.

But I was taken with stillness
& malevolent lords
would eat the living hail
back when I was still blood
intersected by police democrats
were threaded with hell
but I was still coins
like any stupid cuckoo blade
'the baser & poorer sort
such whose lives were burdensome'
I, for example
was quite simply scared
but anyway, inside this language
there is no word for sky

ok, say that again –
the effect is immediate –
no fuss, no bother,
the wind shall blow for evermore:
moan, now
on his white bones
his intolerable name.
He is the man or woman
sitting beside you,
bitter & false & snapped
inside every nation
such hawks & hounds, such ravens
o bitter statistics
the cuckoo is a pretty bird

'yes I wasted my life
on trivialities,
justice, for example,
the pulse of the cities
varied magnetism,
flickers of aged scales,
words shuddered
& the reverie
is a solid thing
burst inside its price
its rainfall, its trembling
hatred is so gentle,
forgive me if I shatter
inside your threads of sleep'

Of gorgeous magnetic fiends
even the memory is blocked:
history's shadow stalks us
call it the net of
the idea is simple
& permanently freakish:
to live outside of servitude
the confidence & cowardice
of those who force us
into fiction, difficult & locked.
But the scorn we feel
BANG
night of the living dead
all else is annoyance & avarice.

In this one night hotel
we've got, you know
the poem –
calculated & horrible,
calculated
& swinging low (o sweet,
with a ribbon in my hair,
a coffin in his throat,
a black boat gliding slow:
everything I need, the
city scorched, in flattering tides
we've got, you know, the poem
glides in slow:
a bitter scream inside this night

black is the colour of my
gestural forthrightness –
gently drops the rain
cold blows the wind:
in May 1968, most
young people were working in
Woolworth's, the cosmetics counter
was so adventurous, a
cloister of learning &
trust, all was represental –
cold / blows the future
ballads of the
BLANK
my true love

if I were like city girls
with few enquiries
transformed into normality
RED ETC
some call it the road to heaven.
Goodbye / sweethearts & pals,
a word of explanation
in preternatural rain, grazing
on the passer-by's
gestures & curses
inside statistical
seven, singing like thrushes
when sickness / came to our
execrable opinions

an old prophecy
found in a bog,
its been traditional or
call it zombies
singing like thrushes
where scorn was:
if I was like city rain
inside your aged banking
in rent shadow, below
we've got, his bastards
just shot us
everything, in its trembling
transferred to tides, but
we shall have commissions galore.

The most talked about
anxiety, the heresy that
'they' appropriated the words
'my enemies'. really
I can't say it,
'normalise' is easier, or
do your duty, dogs
of saturn, in Poundstretcher
and the sea,
where we were refused,
appropriately, the management
identity, a huge circle
repeating cheap wine
& the moon

recent irruptions of unmeaning
in Kabul etc, where
we have never been,
have made poetry obsolete:
but still my red shoes
would go dancing,
tho not a soul would look out
from the curfew, the
cosmetics counter
everyone knows it,
a sentimental space, purely
some kind of folk song, to
give up all love,
the city hurts when it's broken

poetry, once available
in several sizes
of flip discount menace
before the doors of the mighty
the hounds of capital, unleashed
sobriety, knives & clowns.
But politeness would dictate, now
a specific negation of history's
lame dogs & veterans
the british anarchist movement
on a day-trip to the seaside:
ok, say that again,
flatten the official town,
the poem.

outside the concept
are three little words
ringing inside them
we don't know who
on certain chromatic streets
locked inside Poundstretcher
or the cuckoo / take position:
eat shit poetry snobs /
no, we didn't mean that,
strung from star to star
in all this rough music
inaudibly, a black dot,
a monstrous excrescence
a reasonable point of view

below london town
rattling towers flash
harmonically. not a soul
in the police computer
& all other file-sharing
cinematic wreckage
with a ribbon in my hair
expressed harmonically
as politeness dictates
when I say eat shit
it is just this difficulty
my record collection
all these colonised notes
kill little birds like me

ok, say reverie
secretly swallowed by
SPLAT
ok, false gentlemen,
little knots of hair & moon,
we are in your language,
moaning,
gentle drops of lambs
the bitter scream inside gold,
sitting beside you,
trickling,
your exposed alienations,
& the town is yours
o gasping swine

Housing Benefit ref 400158161:
there will be no violence here,
it is perhaps where that thing,
queen elizabeth,
was practising her derivative magic,
burning like a city, a heretic
or a child, insisting softly
on a private & particular sky,
a credit reference, for example,
spotted with Hackney Road,
the dreadful cries of murdered men,
inside poetry,
composed exclusively
for entirely official numbers.

Last night I lay
in darkened walls –
I sucked his –
I used to whip him
with a turquoise chain
he was a big freak
o enchanting fucking
trickling inside woolworths
its cosmetic flash:
o false egyptians
& english sweethearts,
trapped in un-meaning,
would too eat blood
my lily-white hands

Anyway, back in the
police computer
they are making metonyms,
ambitious ones
intersected by pretty towns
& strings of words
but we are mouths
stupid
stitched into the language
that resting place
for exhausted shoppers
for used opinions
call it the graveyard
o computer

Those who believe
they know how to read
are easily intimidated
I mean right now.
But who is speaking here,
such archaic pleasantry
& insolent noise making
is mere freakish difficulty:
history is those who sit
inside their prepared vocab,
the comfortable ones,
the executioner, especially,
never utters an articulate sound,
quietly gets on with his work.

as I was out walking
our musical voices
split to a single chord
REFERENCE CODE
insert seizure
UNAVAILABLE
insert hope & love
a layered pit of stung starlings
as I was out
'hold me fast & fear me not'
inside the lower city
I would suck their snarling
PARAPHRASE
I would rather be the devil

& then we were letters
thinking cities, even
varied, fierce & gold
but swallowed by events
in rainfall, its tides
& police were talking
in social cheap wine
whose life was ludic
with biting, swallowed
by yuppie reveries,
justice, for example
& simpering passion,
a black & burning pit
half-price in woolworths

'I ain't faking, no no' –
but put a businessman's
girdle round the earth
is a dream deferred
like all protest media
& sected corporate urgency
BANG
its musical voices
BLANK
it is not sexual
their guitar strings
a study in asphyxiation
tightened on the known stars
scrawled out, 'their'

he was a big freak
transformed into normality
all the night through
a specific negation of history
& the sea
where scorn was
recent irruptions of unmeaning
flatter the official town's
insolent noise making
secretly my small thighs
trickling down our
sobriety, pronounced
as their favourite line:
goodbye, sweethearts & pals

the wind shall blow hurt
inside every earth's
cut-price reverie:
INSERT WORLD OF BANKING
OUTSIDE
pretending that people were
sexual gestures & thrushes
GARGLED WITH SWEETHEARTS
I don't eat your duty,
build money with a system
of mystical swine
& social trickling –
insert your heads,
have sucked your poem dead.

if I had a fancy sash
my own true love would
rent me out in earrings
but if I had a ribbon bow
in scratches & numbers
he'd read my mind, with hail
burning like a city's
frozen & vivid dead:
but my method is to fear him,
his scorched & wasted coins,
history's oppressive line,
my thighs
my anarchic scales
oh fucking tide

SET TWO //// FOR PAUL SUTTON

I understand that this is general information
& not a full statement of the law

secret history number
don't / step / on
here is your alphabet
elizabeth windsor
housing benefit ref
cough up & shut up:
here is a room to
here is a serum flight
mouth erased now,
you live in rigged integers
burnt gust globes
you live in fun people
negative numbers
motherfucker

now you go ape
sorry but I feel spit:
now redistribute decades
each insomniac decade
step on fun people
each bursts like a dog
nice dog / nice spark
this is your head on TV
this is the dole, revolving
bright magnetic birds
sweep and soar
this is my frequency
a thin metal screech
non-cognitive

& that's not all:
cough up the alphabet
to one side of axis
the decibel, yeh
burnt number, crackled
just as voices
from 'near silence' to
like, 'all hell', where you
don't / 'people person'
bright magnetic secret
inside speech, from silence
outsourced decades
incorporated what is known
&, as they say, numb

don't
rim / fun / people
value notwithstanding
as least I know I'm a moron
isolated, episodic.
certainly, this is ridiculous
try running it backwards
cancel the landscape
the imagination of racists
insert symbol
rhythmic displacement
christians, bureaucrats
keep taking the pills
benefit thief

this is me revolving
certainly, this is spit
like 'all hell' where birds
prowling dogs
sorry / negative decades
live in it like a racist
this is my silence
big constitutional principle
bright magnetic decibel
nice gravity, nice racist
      YEH
have your say David Cameron
music / movies / games
finance / cars / answers

here is a landscape
here is 'all hell',
the distance between each line
some kind of 'celestial snarl'
redistributes the city
a strange and bitter crop
furnace / numbers / christians
yeh / yeh / yeh:
you reach a fork in the voice,
the gaps between the lines
widen / like a mountain range
or those secret rooms
where the law goes to scream
have your say, o burnt decibel

every morning I take a pill
stops electricity, stops
most things / so imagine
you're a, like, nice person
some shuffling guy bites you
& it's music everywhere
communism, dole scroungers
but we go there for money
everything is shimmering
the gaps in your voice
smoke of the bottomless pit
idiots on sulphur
o bollocks
there goes Thatcher again

the report recommends
rhythmic decades / brightly
scattered in rooms, functions
displaced between 'cities'
secret heads / where
the law goes squealing
its penalties & sanctions
its negative hells
redistribution of people
doing 'something', inside
'birds' / audible insertion
of dole pill, 'privately',
a roaring in my speaking
later, Mr Brown said

think of a sound / stretch it
extract the 'I', extract virtually
everyone / 'you', my enemy
phenytoin sodium
controls all warped reels
gaps in the royal alphabet
like 'fun people' / their gravity
is perfect, no distortion:
a voice / slipped through mine, a
tone control, silent & fearsome
extracts each decade, at
playback, requires no adjustment,
a voice / forks into mine, ahem,
clearly heard / coarse & distorted

meanwhile, back in 'british poetry'
dutiful saline monarchy / like
voice it, here's a burnt person
ringing, puking out its decades
its phenytoin pit / sorry but
it's not my fucking landscape
my sweet non-cognitive pal, yeh
beautiful / o functions, careering
most things / cars, heads / o 'you',
            COUGH
finance recommends / speaking pills,
someone's city in pretty flames
            COUGH
'birds' / 'nice sanction' / 'nice decade'

& then there's the side effects –
for starters the skin spreads,
sidesteps the brain dutifully
bends to its own symbolic self
redistributed / knotted / closing
its vision canal, entryway to
doctor or cop or whatever
the prescription parses you
diagonally, & you feel it
as barricades / internalised
masked up / sloganised
a lawful voice on distort gap
in the housing alphabet, a
public service / description

they should hand out guns
on the dole / we don't know
who 'they' are, I have asked
the police, the landlord, but
I cannot leave, who I am
the taxpayer, the violence
of what is called a bully
so I shot them, 'they', the
taxpayer, the landlord / I am
a child & it is a statement, of
sorts, in the language of
that death. & I cannot leave:
the police emptied the content
that white / trembling / meat

I have been studying the process
whereby you become a law
its circuits its interruptions
I swallowed it 17 times
with burning sugar / it was boring
dancing like a murdered cop
his change in circumstances
countercrackling, hobbled
it swallowed him 17 times
asked for an explanation
a system of ancient flinching
ha, mechanicals
you will have to pay it back
from the future, crack'd

'move along, 'fun people',
nothing to see here'
you will have shimmering
a language of the barricades
yeh, I know, sorry
at least I know
who we're working for
running thru its prescriptions
its ancient answers, you
my enemy, doing 'something',
the police, doing 'the alphabet'
its secret monarchy, its meaning
its nice dog functions,
its corporate poetry sucks.

this book has been specially
in clear, non-technical
hordes of palaces, empty
tone controls, a lawful 'you'
inside your word for 'gasoline'
peaks in high-frequency
gusts, bright magnetic scroungers
& the bottomless landlord,
viewed from 15 millivolts, bright
slogans of ancient anaglyphs, bright
wow & flutter / I said non-technical
inaudible to all with lawful hearing,
my silent boring dancing,
oh my, my bare arse flashing

we are Elizabeth Windsor
controlled by a centrifugal
motor shaft / sorry, I mean
I have eaten the taxes
you were saving for / and then
I ate the slave / sorry, I
mean my hips were wriggling:
the rest of this letter
has been returned to you,
it is offensive and inappropriate
controlled by a / sorry
even if I am shot dead,
we will remember these moments
so delicious, for example, so

hello, o burnt frequency
where my eyes were
without a city wall
I have been designing
a new geography of delight
clean & troubled, like
a baby's cry –
flap your knees apart
my insipid drunks, my
shuffling laws, inside
the jerking melting bellies
of detectives & diagrams
such irritating spheres
get up now, dead man

have your say, o disappeared
or non-existent elements, or
our bodies are still here
burning globes / eclipsed:
o shit, I just ate the economy
THAT'S RIGHT
it was a thin metal revolving
so stupid & dying
like a businessman, squealing
like the rats that were left
on our doorstep this morning
that's right / now we know
we are geometric gaps
in police lines / so tender, so

so what, I wasn't talking
for 'you', o functions.
This is how we speak
to our fathers / with lawful
description, they are audible
persons, listen
this is what they taught me,
here are decades, rats that snarl
in clear & ancient taxes
SIMPLE FAMILIAR SENTIMENTS
o scroungers, o gasoline
there's a home for you here
there's a room for your things
me, I like pills / o hell.

yeh well, please don't say
our lives are defeated
just don't / meanwhile
in the past, like in all bright
slogans, they are building
ok, sorry
YEH, EMPATHY
'nice dog' / 'nice dad'
'lets all do the' / o how I love
your language, & lie in it
with all my bare-arsed money
NOTHING
'I laugh when they weep'
'I weep when they laugh'

serene in the fields, like flowers
doing our tax returns / listen
these ringing geometric gaps
have forked our voice, these
O, CANCELLED
anyway, let's imagine seven doves
encircle your speaking, let's unload
YEH / YEH / YEH
encircled secret voice
like 'all hell', your name has gnawed
SHUT UP
a ringing conducting medium
invisibility amassed at the border
my cupid heart is shattered

'my work takes me out of town'
THEY'RE ALL DEAD IN THEIR HOUSES
o dog inside my voice, inside
distorted frequencies, wild cell
where our love sits troubled
& described / but they're still dead
'my work' / o bright gasoline, my
lawful voice. Flap your knees apart
COUGH
or, if you like, your brittle mouth
COUGH
to live in these charred places
walls of grief will devour us
dreams & faces / distorted roads

hello, sweet & distant voice
my decrepit moon & law /
you know, from this angle
the average british landlord
with his non-existent numbers
his voltage & his arson / typically
on simple 'nice person' circuits
goes to dinner most days
sends doves through the post
is, at least, a very good fuck
this is where I scream
SORRY
the police lines between us
have raised a thicket of beetles

61 wide-eyed numbers
falling out of the sky
sign em, they are your
efforts to find work
help em, they are deaf
but lawful, tumbling
from the slats of the sky
crows, not cuckoos, crows
lepers, evidence, cars
bright magnetic whistling
this is your jobsearch
FRIENDS
here is the village you ordered
we burned its houses down

the secondary dole office
situ 656A Forest Road
(E17) / is the planet's rim
quite obviously, its
opprobrious contempt & fire
barely conceals / a false wall
to rack the noises, a
presumably rich city, a
WAKE UP / you are here
informed, via 2 or 3 nights
of sincere sleep deprivation
& bitter funds / the poem
is merely an arrest warrant
'A' is not equal to 'A'

SET THREE

the starving are beginning to know the way
to your great cafés and restaurants

I wish London would
like, you know,
but then again
I'm one of its noises
or rather, its noose.
nah, just kidding, yeh,
one of the pavements
is all, spiral chatter, am
eating the voices
the interval cracks
the crossroads, yeh
real devil business
& the cops are there
we crucified em

& the moon / remember that
there are people on it
& they have married us
weird, those consummations
those noises that waken us
roaring & absurdly whistling
& it frightens us
there's so many of them
curled around us, inaudible
the ages, history, entire galaxies
they are eating us
citizens of raided spheres
the sky / red as a burning flag
a supreme vodka / treacherous stars

who here can speak
the language of the dead
what they meant to say
I wanna be your dog
THE RADIO IS LEAKING
they know they're dead
yeh / & they're not scared
chewing up the language
AS I WAS OUT WALKING
obscurely thru their brains
those thin metal spheres
subterranean rooms
when I was a country girl
going down to the drugstore

meanwhile, there are voices
glazed ones, rectangular ones
are trickling down our thighs
into swarms of cancelled centuries
anxious ones / FUSES
each one lives a double life
paupers, vagabonds, criminals
FUSES / FUSES / FUSES
Yeh, well, not to worry
they have no legs to walk on
they have no mouth to speak with
it's 11.58 in London
contact us immediately
THE METAL DISCS OF THE SUN

or, from another angle
thought this was paradise
bone of my speechless bone
or rather, london pavements
clasped & wrapped, contained
your era, my stilettos / or
revolving spheres, whatever
it's 11.58, whatever that means
tame jackals, springing fools
from a different perspective
we are your dead coins
your glazed leather beds
'how old are you, my –'
noises / noises / noises

but in the claims made by music
posterity is leaking, strangely
tucked in minor constellations
strangely radiant executives
flatterers / amnesiacs / nouns
polite ones, yeh, rushing ideas
in a tame feather bed. but no,
we weren't talking to you
say 'iradium', say '1917'
say 'the books of the future
cracking the brain of the past'
no, don't say that, it's stupid
those people on the moon,
we left em there, plainly singing

anyway, here in the multiplex
in our plastercasts / in in
in our membranes, like, inside
the police computer, that thing
ok / inside our medicines
trickling down our thighs
our crossroads our whistling
inside like cracks / dogs / brains
'last night in a warm feather bed
that's right, the cold cold ground
is eating us / we, cancelled criminals
so warm inside the police etc
fucking set fire to cars etc
little birds, nothing / I mean

so we were buying weapons
ok / let's start that again –
on public transport, it happened
we were sitting opposite
bullets / chemistry / glass
we were separated. inside
what we once were. & they
were sitting opposite, empirical
& scared. they were scared
of us / our charts & remorse
no-one knows / we were buying
inside their office, the dead
they were scared of us, of
our seven metals / & radar shrike

but as I was out walking
with the strange & bitter men
we were / say it / we were
anxious radar dogs / we were
oblivious swarms, cancelled
solvents, polite ones / we were
a confused mass of centuries
seven burning circles / were
electrons / proverbs / molecules
from hand to crackling hand
a fraudulent cosmology
a hole in the ground
I wish london would
like, crack its face / o cuckoo

here in Poundstretcher / we are
BLANK
we are building nebulae, falling
like, I dunno, wages / but anyway –
'how old are you, my
sweet critique of poetry
burning, prize-winning factory.
True, we were entire galaxies
but now it's 11.58 in London
it's AM & PM, both. No point
in waking your oblivious storms
I mean in Poundstretcher
ten thousand were drowned
on discount / cosy & warm

but ghosts are necessary
a chart of / a collective
inarticulate harmony
item: minor surface noise
item: a basement strata
its bibliographic shell
I mean, its celestial arc
has got us surrounded.
Anyway, here in 1917
we're having a right laugh
no point in waking you
love's solar boat is slashed
is trickling down our thighs
the chatter of the past

meaning, the surface sector
or London, just sitting there
we're not criminals, no
but the dead are, inaudible
these songs of burning circles
& then we saw medicines
trickling down our world
its membranes & posterity
weird, this springing speech
was blood in another circuit
not ours tho, so whatever
crackling in our tombs
we are warm & empirical
when we're frightened, we

in this recent knot of days
the vile prickle of pills
is entirely political / these
grimy days, yeh, their static
preposterous symmetry / so
the side effects are, well
like this: it's 11.58, precisely
an entire molecular assembly
a ring of executive flats
a cheap solar monopoly. But,
I dunno, from another angle,
PITCHED GREEN MALEVOLENCE
OF THE ENGLISH COUNTRYSIDE
o cuckoo, nasty little churches

anyway / I just ate the passer-by
via 2 or 3 executive crossroads
known as burning talk / concealed
in the claims made by finks
their preposterous symmetry
strange, flattering numbers / but
COUGH
but as I was out walking, through
our musical positions, we were
sweethearts & membranes
we were sorry and tasteless
we were trickling curfews, but
here, safe inside our offices
we are eating / yes / & feeding

meanwhile, we were documentaries
a code made of letters, like
unaroused by official culture.
For some reason, it was 1649,
we were trapped inside it, clutching
our most reasonable point of view.
I can't say more / vast territories
of our singing selves, decommissioned.
Maybe it was 2003, or something,
I don't remember, my favourite laws
were just a system of false brains
I recognise that / splintered & oblique
social utterance flaming malevolence
magnetic, would soon go dancing etc

our minds are clean & pleasant
BLISS
listen, we are your friends
BLANK
gliding like magazines / we
inside each nation's serenity
sitting near you on the bus
totally harmless characters
strange and flattering numbers
seriously, trickling inside
what we once were / we
esoteric in panic
swifter than birds
in our social role, objects –

objects / tobacco & brandy
or something truly ridiculous
class struggle / in poetry also
YAWN
its contagion is spread
via rhymesters, their embers
their swarms of bone
not zombies, sirens
criss-cross a fraudulent
a map of, of what –
got an art council grant
will burn their houses down
YAWN
everyone's been buried alive

anyway, eclipse, as I was –
although we live in the city
SO
they wouldn't arrest us, their
astrology / starkly inside us.
It was a contented era, a
justification. They could not
arrest / their threads & names.
anyway, I owe this reference to
CERTAIN INTERNATIONAL EVENTS
CERTAIN CONFORMITIES
it was 1974 / a ballad recalls /
'the life which once I had
by law is now controlled'

but / here in socialist realism
its musical ferrotypes / its
its reversal narratives / its
AS IN
'in London where we dwell
is a burning we know full well'
ITS ANCIENT TRANSPOSITIONS
those noises flaming / in birds
notes we were squealing in
CUCKOOS & BIRDS
as in the alphabet's bandits
ITS CENTRIFUGAL WINDOWS
CELLS, SECTIONS, GROUPS
ITS OFFICIAL PARENTS BROKEN

posterity / landlord / spheres
swarms / jobsearch / wind
WOW, LAWS
eclipse / reverie / slaves
magnetic / scholar / finks
o millivolt / o globe
THIS IS A
FLASHING like
we are ringing geometrics
a tame & trickling noise
curfew / playback / disks
singing like violence
my true love
my black & speechless bone

this lecture was brought to
by typical silence & gold / it is
YOU KNOW, LIKE A HYPHEN
I'VE ROBBED YOUR POOR
Anyway, in 1649
YOUR POOR POCKETS
not alphabets, fissures
YEH I KNOW, BROKEN
YOUR SILVER & GOLD
'on sundays often strolled
to have their fortune –
THIS LECTURE HAS BEEN
IN THESE WILD DESERTS
weirds had warped us, so

we closed / we are inside
YOUR OPINIONS
YOUR MEMBRANES FLASHING
we are compliant & broken
we are gardens of silence
THE DEAD, SO POLITELY
IN OUR PETTICOATS
IN OUR BALLADS OF
'got the devil in my soul'
'& I'm full of bad booze'
THE STILLNESS
SUCH SPARKLING FLIGHT
history is those who
the seagulls / the

anyway, now we were centuries
sort of had faces / we encircled
DREAMLESS, MUTED DECIBELS
OUR TREATIES / THE VISIBLE
we scratched our faces off
our references, lines of credit
A KIND OF GLOW REMAINS
A KIND OF DIGNIFIED SINGING
BLANK
meanwhile, in the drugstore
BLANK
we are your border
BRIGHT
INAUDIBLE

LETTERS AGAINST THE FIRMAMENT

Because such people stand in violent circumstances
their language too, almost in the manner of the furies,
speaks in a nexus of more violent connections.

HÖLDERLIN

I think it was probably some kind of terrible mistake. He'd howl all through the night, bloodshot and ridiculous: 'I am not to blame. Prison, slavery, luxury. Crowbars and magistrates. Metaphors and factories'. I didn't know what he expected from me: his thought-processes were mysterious, his logic slightly disturbing, all I could do was laugh in his face. Each morning I would clamber out the window, and wander through a landscape of geometrical music, a galaxy of vaguely corrosive stereotypes. State bureaucrats, military prisons. I had compressed all centuries, the better to see into his bones, the insipid cultural signals that had bound us together so strangely.

Sleep was no better. I'd turn out the light and his voice would be all that remained, rumbling like an imageless space, like surgery, an immense collection of shattered and pilfered hours. His idiotic dreams cut through me at impossible angles, finance and real estate shredded and negated. We had been walking together for centuries, sucking on stones, on cavern gas, on corked wine and planetary diagrams. I had meant it as a kindness: to tear out his heart, throw it to the dogs and to the homeless. The songs of heaven, the secrets of history, the kidnap and murder of David Cameron. Steal away.

I'm spending most of my time hungry these days. A real hunger; sharp, greedy and endless. Sometimes I have to stay in bed all day because of it, this maddening weakness, hollow nausea. I bet you think I'm exaggerating. So fuck you. OK, I'm sorry, that was a bit rude. I'll try and explain what I mean by 'fuck you'. The High Street. Walthamstow, or anywhere else. Everyone gazing at their reflections in all of the empty shop windows, weird technicians digging up the pavements. Don't think this is delirium, or paranoia. Well maybe it is, but maybe that doesn't matter. The perceptual shifts related to hunger as a means of interpretation. Hunger as beginning of thought. So bear with me. All of those empty shops, full zombie, the absolute calendar. Comedy. History. Masks and plague sores. Mass renunciation, reactionary weather systems, everything. As if the world had shuddered and a massive, spiralling Medusa had scampered through some cheap sci-fi wormhole and was biting us to death. Swallowing and biting. The shop windows, the reflections, are the only hiding place, the only escape. And don't think I'm getting all mythological on your ass. Try to understand that Medusa to be simply the accumulated historical pressure of pure bullshit, or molecules and radio gas, all of it forming a mass intracranial solid neoplasm that, if decoded, may at least give us some sense, the beginnings of an actual map, of what we have to do to reach the next stage – the first stage, it feels like – of what some people still rather quaintly refer to as 'the struggle'. Yeh, I know, I'm one of those people. Sometimes my vocabulary makes me cringe. But if those shop windows, those reflections operate as some kind of safety valve, then they are also, put simply, the visible points of an inverted world nailed onto this one, violent, unresting, an insect system where each abandoned hour of what was once called 'socially necessary labour time' becomes detached, on its own orbit, like some absolute planet, but habitable, the way an abandoned office space or a derelict private home is habitable. It turns the city inside out. We become property, pure and simple, with no disguises. And so we rent ourselves out, we got no choice. We become derelict storefronts, vacant buildings, fire-traps. We rent ourselves out to a pack of corporate tenants, glass sapphires and enemy systems. Starbucks etc. Just to be obvious. Tesco. A ratpack, sitting there, inside us, eating. All the while eating. Ah, maybe it's not so bad. Maybe we can use it, this hunger, this coded swarm. To get a sense of what the murderously rotational teeth of a key, for example, actually mean. To understand what eating actually is. To know what biting is, and subsumption. To understand the secret secular fuck-toys of the entire social labyrinth to be a simple sheet of buckling and starving glass. A brick through the window. A message. And all of that is pretty much what I mean when I use the words 'fuck you'. But anyway, that's not why I'm writing. Like the ghost I've become, I'm now looking for a job, and I was hoping you'd write me a reference. You'll do it, of course, I know it.

For sale. Everything the management dictated. Celestial dirt and the western scale. The victory of the sailors at Kronstadt. The victory of the miners at Orgreave. The odour of sanctity. Fictional factories. Special discounts on bossnappings, modern landlords and the seekers of lice.

For sale. Top people of all descriptions. Chewing lice, sucking lice, bird-lice. The victory of the rioters at Poundland. Ed Miliband fucked by lice. The defect in the law and the dream deferred. Cameron as nightingale. For sale. Wrapped in wire and torched. For sale. The gospel of saving and abstinence. The victory of the Mau Mau at St James' Palace. Infrageography. Microtomes. Tactical spectrums. Sudden harmony and affliction. The corrosive victory of the unemployed. A carbomb for the DWP.

So I guess by now you'll have recovered from the voodoo routines at St Paul's. Guess it's nice that we won't have to pronounce the syllables Margaret Thatcher again. It all seems very distant now, like when you've been up for four nights, finally get some sleep, and then you're sitting there drinking a cup of coffee trying to remember what the hell you've been up to. You still know that feeling? You'd better. Anyway, the thing I remember most clearly is Glenda Jackson's speech in parliament, when all the rest of them were wittering on about Thatcher and God and the entire fucking cosmos and there was Jackson laying out a few home truths. But really, it's a measure of the weirdness of those few days how fearless that speech seemed: and, obviously, a measure of the weirdness that it actually was some kind of act of bravery. Tho the best bit was when the anonymous Tory MP started wailing 'I can't stand it' in the middle of it. Like, that's right, motherfucker. Anyway, so I listened to Jackson's speech on Youtube a few times, and then I went and checked her voting record in parliament – bit of a letdown, yeh. Abstained on the workfare vote, yeh. So that's her, she can fuck off. She made a much better speech back in 1966, I think it was, playing Charlotte Corday in the film of Peter Weiss's *Marat/Sade* – I guess you remember it, she's up at the top of a ladder, going off her head, and screaming something along the lines of 'what is this city, what is this thing they're dragging through the streets?'. Christ, if she'd done that in parliament, I might have rethought my relationship with electoral politics. Well, maybe not. But seriously, what was that thing they were dragging through the streets on April 17th, or whatever day it was. Through that silenced, terrified city. I thought of Thatcher as some kind of rancid projectile, and they were firing her back into time, and the reverberations from wherever it was she landed, probably some time in around 1946, were clearly a more-or-less successful attempt to erase everything that wasn't in a dull, harmonic agreement with whatever it is those razorhead vampire suckworms in parliament are actually trying to do with us. Firing us into some kind of future constructed on absolute fear. Or that future is a victorious vacuum, a hellish rotating disc of gratuitous blades, and they are speaking to you, those blades, and what they are saying is this: 'one day you will be unemployed, one day you will be homeless, one day you will become one of the invisible, and monsters will suck whatever flesh remains on your cancelled bones'. They're not kidding. And the grotesque and craggy rhythms of those monsters are already in our throats, right now. In our throats, our mouths, the cracked centre of our language, fascist syllables, sharp barking. You know I'm not exaggerating. What they're planning is nothing small. We're talking about thousands of years, their claws extending into the past and into the future. A geometrical city of forced dogs, glycerin waves, gelignite. And what a strange, negative expression of the scandalous joy we were all feeling, at the death-parties, pissed out of our heads in Brixton, in Trafalgar Square, all of those sites of ancient disturbances suddenly blasted wide apart. A pack of Victorian ghosts. Nights of bleeding and electricity. Boiling gin and police-lines. White phosphorous. Memories. It was like we were a blister on the law. Inmates. Fancy-dress jacobins. Jesters. And yes. Every single one of us was well aware that we hadn't won anything, that her legacy 'still lived on', and whatever other sanctimonious spittle was being coughed up by liberal shitheads in the *Guardian* and on Facebook. That wasn't the point. It was horrible. Deliberately so. Like the plague-feast in *Nosferatu*. I loved it. I had two bottles of champagne, a handful of pills and a massive cigar, it was great. I walked home and I wanted to spray-paint 'Never Work' on the wall of every Job Centre I passed. That's right, I'm a sentimental motherfucker when I'm out of my head. But no, already that foul, virtuous fear was sinking back into me, taking possession of my every step. I was thinking about Blanqui, right at the end of his life, sitting in his prison cell, knowing full well that what he was writing he was going to be writing for ever, that he would always be wearing the clothes he was wearing, that he would always be sitting there, that his circumstances would never, ever change. How he couldn't tell the difference between his prison cell and the entire cluster of universes. How the stars were nothing but apocalypse routines, the constellations negative barricades. I was thinking about the work-ethic, how it's evoked obsessively, like an enemy ritual, some kind of barbaric, aristocratic superstition. About zero-hours contracts, anti-magnetic nebulae sucking the working day inside out. Negative-hours. Gruel shovelled into all the spinning pits of past and future centuries, spellbound in absolute gravity, an in-visibility blocking every pavement I was walking down. I wanted to cry. In fact I think I did. Actually, no. I was laughing my head off. A grotesque, medieval cackle. No despair, just defiance and contempt. Ancient disturbances. Ghost towns and marching bands. Invisible factories. Nostalgia crackling into pain and pure noise. No sleep. No dreams. An endless, undifferentiated regime of ersatz work. All of us boiled down into some stupid, Tory alarm clock. A ringing so loud we can no longer even hear it. But whatever. It seems pretty obvious we should adopt the Thatcher death-day as some kind of workers' holiday. Actually, scratch that, let's just celebrate it every day, for ever and ever, like a ring of plague-sores, botulism and roses. A barbaric carnival of rotten gold and infinite vowels. Sorcery. Rabies. You know what I mean? I hope so. Anyway, things have been pretty quiet since then. I've been thinking about paying you a visit. Oh shit.

LETTER AGAINST FEAR (UNSENT)

I don't quite know how to say this. A couple of nights ago I had some kind of terrible dream. I don't remember anything about it, not the narrative, not anything, just a sense of black beating wings at the centre of, well, everything. Perhaps there was no narrative, or rather, only the flipside, as if I was hanging from it, from all the threads and unrevealed disclosures, the nets of place dangling, a sublime matrix I was, well, choking inside. The Surrealists were wrong, obviously: there's no 'marvellous' in the dream, it runs diagonally through your body, like that lightning rod that spears Patrick Troughton in *The Omen*. You know the bit, yeh. He's running through the churchyard, some kind of storm, some kind of panic weather – I don't remember very clearly, I haven't seen it since I was a kid. Anyway, just as he reaches the church, his work-place, whatever, the lightning rod at the top of the spire, or is it a weather-vane, I dunno, it plummets forward, snaps off, and it spears him. Rivets him to the ground, and to time. That's what a dream is. That's what it signals, some kind of policed rift, some kind of brutal radio wave, where everything you've ever feared or loved or both is compressed into one infinitely dense anti-magnetic spike, an anti-magnetic barricade, and you are left there, fixed into place, dangling there, trapped, like some kind of imaginary animal. Sorry. That's pretty depressing. But I woke up out of it at 3 that morning, and I haven't been able to sleep since. I got up and paced around in horrible circles, couldn't stop. I haven't felt like that since, you remember, we mainlined all of that ridiculous speed, and it wasn't fun, all of our talk shattered into spirals of dust, and we decided we could see the 'world spirit', and, well, I dunno. Like a perfumed rapture turned inside out: the city as rat-trap, as unreconciled bondage and chicken-wire. Anyway, thanks for your letter. I think your ideas about psychogeography are idiotic, actually. I can't believe you ever took that shit seriously. I mean, yeh, obviously, the city is a giant clock, but still, I would have thought the recent explosions, the networks of racist attacks and so forth, would have made you adjust your interpretations just a little. How the hell do you think we can read the silent workings of the city's risible little head via slightly exotic walking tours, table-tapping and ghost stories. Like, we're the fucking ghosts, yeh. It's the signals from the future I'm interested in. I dunno, maybe it's different for you. The fact you get paid, I guess, the fact that you're on a salary, does give you a point of entry that, for the time being at least, I don't really have access to. To be unemployed is to be a stowaway, at best. From where I'm sitting, all I can hear is a dull metronomic beating, sentimental rants about extermination and terror and the like. What are the psychogeographical signals set off by a fascist mob, for example, what galaxies and rhythmic swarms are they colliding with. Absolute magnetic compressions. History as a separable particle, a damp electric rag shoved down our kidnapped throats. I dunno, maybe I'm wrong. I wish you'd tell me. I wish you were capable of saying just one word that would convince me all narrative structures – including those of the so-called avant garde – haven't been reduced to something as basic as a crowbar, a massive memory lapse, a constellation of chemical dirt and bizarre melodies that no-one is dancing to. Sorry, I can't get to whatever it is I'm trying to say. I daren't, in fact. Every day I leave the house at least once, to go for a walk. Usually it's just to the supermarket, but sometimes I go as far as the railway tracks. It's all overgrown down there, it's kind of peaceful. A damp landscape of rust and brambles, where the signal-towers and voices can begin to seem like the components of some barely remembered dream. And actually, now I can remember, that was the dream I was trying to tell you about, that was its structure, that was all it was. I was in an abandoned station house. The silence was endless. And then I woke up. There was some kind of ticking in the corner of the room. I couldn't tell what it was. I couldn't see to switch on the light. What was that ticking. Why did it sound like it was coming from the centre of my chest. Why was I so helpless and afraid.

LETTER AGAINST SICKNESS

> One is happy enough when in these agitated times one can take
> refuge in the depth of tranquil passions
>
> GOETHE

Couldn't sleep again last night. Someone had paid for a couple of nights in a hotel, down by the coast, I've no idea why, or who, for that matter. I sat there for hours, nervous, watched the rolling news with the sound down, inventing my own dialogue like I used to do when I was a kid. Anyway, George Osborne came up, his little mouth moving at unpleasant angles and, weirdly, it occurred to me that I couldn't remember what his voice sounded like. Not sure why, I mean I've heard it often enough. So I thought, masochistically or not, that I ought to remind myself: I turned the volume up and just as I did he was saying the words 'our NHS'. The weight that pronoun carried was unbearable. Because Osborne, who presumably doesn't actually use the NHS, who probably has never sat in a waiting room in, say, the Whipps Cross Hospital, was claiming some kind of possession that was entirely stolen, and claiming to share it with some kind of absolutely occupied 'us'. It changed everything: the bland hotel room, the banal beating of the sea, all of it congealed into Osborne's pronunciation of 'our'. There was a sickness to it that hung far outside the radius of any hospital. A vacant pestilence, or, if you like, a bricked-up pestilence, and the 'us', which itself was some kind of shattered twitching mass left over from Osborne's thrusting invasion of 'our', this 'us' was in hopeless distant orbit around this pestilence, some kind of arrangement of speckles in the night sky, a more or less orderly glyph, a surgical fracture in celestial time and, well, I guess you know what I mean. It did my head in, and the sun was starting to come up, so I thought I'd go out for a walk. And the first thing I saw, when I walked out the hotel door, was a seagull eating a pigeon. Serious. Right there in the middle of the road, tearing it to strips, swallowing the motherfucking thing. There was nobody around. Just the sea, some pebbles. And this peculiar compressed violence I was staring at. I couldn't move. I just stood there, staring, wishing I could reduce it down to some kind of metaphor, or analogy, or starting point for a bit of bourgeois literary criticism, something to add to my CV, anything, rabies, anything. The gull, the pebbles, pronouns, the rolling news, the sea, the dead thing, all of them forming into some kind of knot or eclipse. I thought about you at this point. I wondered which of them you would identify with. Which part would you take in this little horrorshow, which would be the marker of your position, which would be your representative on earth, which would be your signature. I ask because I really don't know which one I would be. I mean, if George Osborne was lying there in tatters in the middle of the road, right in front of the ridiculous sea, would I eat him? I'm sort of serious. If I walked out of the hotel and he was lying there, whimpering like a burning dog, what would I do? Shit, I was sweating by this point. I was no longer even a human being, just some glowing monster of anxieties and vicious isotopes, storms and circles. Revenge. Law. Decency. I think I puked. I felt I had become a tiny fissure in the decay chain set off by George Osborne's voice. One among countless disinterested scalpels, hanging there, in the grains of his voice. And those scalpels are us. Anyway, I couldn't take it. I crossed the road and went down to the beach. I'm still here. I wrote you this letter, but I probably won't send it. If I do, do not answer it.

with his knees and his fists in bituminous black

GARCÍA LORCA

ok think this / or as in scabies, social ones
in any fiscal exit, in any skaldic bullet glass
is spinning: like the scorn of andromeda
would compress our picket cells, as infinite
scratch that / with all your social nails, like
literally, inside our cutting waters, nails, like
inside our stuttered fall / & capital is mind
o frozen predicate: as in any social microbe
is mundane and berserk, as any slave ship, as
any social drunken boat, as in any scabrous
general strike, o scarab: would scratch this
numbered surface bone / like our finite scorn
of prison nails / this thing has fourteen lines
as in picket lines / like venus in a closing sky

I haven't written for a while, I know. There's not been much to write about, or maybe, if there has been I haven't seen it. That's leaving aside, of course, the royal birth, the jubilee pageants and the olympics, that inbred panegyric. Christ, I've really felt the wings of imbecility passing over me lately, over all of us. It's as if the ruling class, sheer power, whatever you want to call it, whatever it's local franchise likes to call itself, had, via some kind of sadistic alchemy, taken the moment (around 2 in the afternoon) on 27th March 2011 when the Black Bloc had gone running up Oxford Street, and had basically erased that moment, replaced it with a long and uninteresting parade of babies, flags, cupcakes, brooms, victims, mummifications, the UKBA on every street corner, their guns, their illegal warrants, their racial profiles and problem families, and their scabs. I thought this morning that I might be able to pull it together for you, this immense shift in the immediate social atmosphere, this peculiar tectonic whitewash – I thought I might be able to pull it together as some kind of wondrous mathematics, a monumental calculus, but I can't get it to fit. Because, for example, if you take the forced removal of the homeless from all commercial zones within the city, multiply that by the statistical weight of the key dates of any given revolutionary narrative, each of which is then to be inserted, almost like an experimental flu virus, into the generalised chronology of whatever century this is supposed to be, if you take that and divide it by the approximate half-life of all occupied buildings and street-fires recorded over the last, I don't know, half century, and from that extrapolate the given name of every person suicided since the new welfare regulations were introduced, extrapolate those names and place them inside a small box built of absolute plutonium, i.e. the sheer terror all of us have started to feel at every unexpected knock at the door, if you do all of this you may be able to get at least some kind of sense of what has actually been done to all of us over the past couple of years, because after a while, say for example a month, those names will have been, via some kind of corporate alchemy, transformed into the manufacture, sale and distribution of third degree burns, multiple organ failure and tiny droplets of phosphoric acid, mostly for overseas distribution, obviously, but the same ingredients can also be boiled down for the home market, boiled down and transformed into an infinitely dense, attractively coloured pill which, upon ingestion, makes the whole city seem like a golden swarm of dragonflies and pretty moths, in which the latest royal baby can somehow pretend not to be an injection of homeopathic rabies into the speaking abilities of each and every one of us, and in which the street value of each of these pills can be taken to equal the external force of the ancient city walls considered as a rudimentary and absolutely incomprehensible incendiary device, and those walls are made of silver, which is cut with sulphur and arsenic, and those walls are of gold, which is made from sand and dust, and those walls are of mercury, which is unsuitable for making coins, and those coins are of piss and phosphor, each in compliance with international law. It would, of course, be a very partial calculation. So much for maths as an algebraic counterforce to capital's tedious little multiplication tables, it keeps coming out more like an oracular scattering of starling bones, of meat and shrieking larks. The place and the formula, as Rimbaud called it. 16th July 2013, for example. Or June 6th 1780. Or 6th October 1985. All the constellations of the royal bastard. Oh murdered London, the city of Mark Duggan. We, the servants of dogs. And you ask me why I don't write poetry. As if a metaphor could actually be a working hypothesis, and not just a cluster of more-or-less decorative alibis. I can't do it. I haven't slept since Thatcher. Curses on the midnight hag.

I think I'm becoming slightly unwell. I've developed a real fear of the upstairs neighbours. Every morning they emit a foul stench of bitumen and bitter, moral superiority as they stomp through the corridor on their way to work. A while ago I told you I rarely leave the house, now I can't, they've spun a web of 9 to 5 self-worth across the door, a claim on the law, moebus claws. I'm trapped. I keep the curtains closed. Don't answer the phone. Panic when the mail's delivered. I don't know if this is normal behaviour, if anyone else feels the city as a network of claws and teeth, an idiot's hospital, a system of closed cameras and traffic. I'm probably beginning to smell. In fact I know I am: a thick cloud of inaudible noises from upstairs, dank growlings from somewhere outside the ring of the city. I feel I'm being menaced by judges. Who the hell are they. What are they doing inside me. I can't hear their voices, but each chain of wordforms solidifies inside my throat, inside my mouth, inside my own voice. It is no articulate sound. It is as if every verb had coagulated into a noun, and the nouns themselves transformed into something subterranean, blind and telescopic. I don't know if I can even see. I think I injected my eyes with gold one night, or at least the idea of gold, some kind of abstraction, and ever since then I've only sensed the city, as a wave of obsolete vibrations and omens. The gold itself some kind of anachronism, a dull rock rolling backwards into whatever remains of historic time. Each time-unit manufactured by a sweatshop suicide somewhere on the other side of the planet. The entire history of London, from its origins as an occultist trading post right up to some point in the not so distant future when it will be inevitably sucked into the spinning guts of Kronos and, well. All of that manufactured by sweatshop suicides, the kind of people my upstairs neighbours will insist over and again simply do not exist. But what do they know? Each evening I hear them, walking around, stomp-stomp-stomping, tap-tap-tapping out their version of social reality on their floor, on my ceiling. It's terrible. And since I can't even leave the flat anymore, the ceiling might as well be the whole of the sky, and they're tapping out new and brutal constellations. Here's the sign of the surveillance camera. Here's the medusa. Here's the spear of Hades. Here's the austerity smirk. Here's the budget. A whole new set of stars. Astrology completely rewritten. It's like they're the sun and the moon, or the entire firmament, a whole set of modernized, streamlined firmaments. What fucking asswipes.

the wealthier homes
have occupied my voice
can say nothing now, yes
my language has cracked
is a slow, creaking fire
deadens my eyes, in
high, contorted concern
fuses to protein and rent

I know. I'd been hoping to spare you any further musings I might have had on the nature of Iain Duncan Smith, that talking claw. But perhaps we're at a point now where we need to define him, to recite and describe, occupy his constellations. Because to recite the stations of the being of Iain Duncan Smith, as if they were a string of joy-beads, and they are, would be to recite the history of the law, if we take that law to be something as simple as a mouth is, and each noise, each syllable that emits from that mouth is only ever and never more than the sound of animals eating each other, a gap in the senses where the invisible universe goes to die, and we become like ghosts or insomniacs stumbling through the city, we become the music of Iain Duncan Smith, his origin in the chaos of animals and plants, of rocks and metals and the countless earths, where over and again he breaks children's teeth with gravel-stones, covers them with ashes. Because to classify those stations, the cancer-ladder of the dreams of Iain Duncan Smith might, at a push, be to consume him, and to define those stations, those marks on the hide of Iain Duncan Smith, might be to trap him, to press granite to the roof of his mouth, the stations of the law. And at this point, obviously, I really wish I could think of something to say that was hopeful, that was useful, that was not simply a net of rats blocking the force of the sun, till it crawls on its fists and knees, screaming like a motherfucker, sarcastic and wrathful, boiling the mountains as if they were scars, laughing, laughing like a crucifixion, modular and bleached. Bleached with the guts of Iain Duncan Smith, of each of the modest number of words he actually understands, such as grovel and stingray and throat, chlamydia, wart. And those five words are the entirety of the senses of Iain Duncan Smith, the gates to his city, his recitation of the germs of the law, a clock that never strikes and never stops, where we are not counted, wiped from the knots of statistics, comparable to fine gold, receptacles of song, shrieking gulls. It's all I can bear to listen to, that shrieking. It blocks out the stars, the malevolent alphabet he's been proposing.

because your mouth is bitter
with executioner's salt, perhaps
when you die, perhaps
you will flutter through Hades
invisible, among the scorched dead

may you vanish there, famished
through the known and unknown worlds

Pay it all back. Leave the dead to their natural stations. Burst open the prisons. Roast yourselves, feed yourselves to the beggars. And if you do not do this we will gouge out your eyes. To take from you all you have broken, all you have taken, what you have made of us, of the circuits of the earth, for all of this we will take your eyes from you, and we will save them, as a record of your vision, as a vessel of deceit and dereliction, that no longer will you stalk the earth, no longer will you invent imperious darkness, a darkness we will never forget, as we will never forget you, devourers of the planet earth, we will keep you in our mouths, and we will keep you there to recite the filth of your lives, and we will do this so you roam forever through the known and unknown hells, and we will do this that the endless solar gulls and the endless whirring of the firmament will no longer simply be money, and so the dogs of the beggars will bark and run, like invisible ghosts will feed on your bones in eternal night.

Thanks for your letter. You think I spend too much time going after 'easy targets', do you? Got to admit I chuckled over that one. A while ago, you recall, I admitted to you I make a fetish of the riot form, and in that admission implied I was fully aware of the risks involved, that any plausible poetics would be shattered, like a shop window, flickering and jagged, all of the wire exposed and sending sharp twists and reversible jolts into whatever it was I was trying to explain or talk about. Think about it this way. Imagine that you had a favourite riot, one that you loved. Tottenham. Millbank. Chingford. Walthamstow. I like the last one, but only for senti-mental reasons. It's a stupid question, but maybe will help you to see what I mean when I use the word 'poetics', or 'poetry'. What was Marx referring to when he was talking about the 'poetry of the future', for example? And what use is that in thinking about pros-ody? Anyway. Loads of people have made maps of clusters of riots, trying to come up with some kind of exegesis based on location and frequency. And quite right too. Think of the micro-vectors sketched out within the actions of any individual rioter, of how those vectors and actions relate to those shared among her or his immediate physical group, and thus the spatio-physical being of that group in relation to their particular town / city, and finally, the superimposition of all of those relations in all of their directions and implications onto an equally detailed charting of the entire landmass understood as chronology and interpretation. Christ, you could include data about the weather-systems on Neptune if you wanted to. What would happen to this map, I've been asking myself, if we went on to superimpose the positions of riots of the past, the future too if you want to be facetious, onto the complexi-ties we're already faced with. Sudden appearance of the Baltimore Riots of 1968, to take a random example. Or the Copper Riots of 1662. The Opera Riot, Belgium, 1830. The 1850 Squatters Riot, California. Personally, I like the Moscow Plague Riots of 1771, both for their measures of poetry and analogy, and for the thought of them as an element of the extraordinarily minor Walthamstow Riot of 7th August 2011. Plague is a bad metaphor, that's it accu-racy, it refers to both sides, all sides, in quantitively different ways.

But primarily, it's dirt simple. It runs in both directions. Means both us and them. As in, metaphor as class struggle, also. As decoration for some unspeakable filth, on the one hand, or as working hypothesis on the other. A jagged rip through all pronouns. The thunder of the world, a trembling, a turbine. Cyclical desperation, clusters of walls. The first signs of plague hit Moscow in late 1770, as in a sudden system of forced quarantine and destruction of con-'taminated houses. Within a few months, a clock of vast scratching, fear and anger. September 15th they invaded the Kremlin, smashed up the monastery there. The following day they murdered the Archbishop, that wormfucker, Ambrosius, they killed him, and then torched the quarantined zones. Much burning, yeh, much gunshot and vacuum. And no antidote, no serum. Around 200,000 people died, not including those who were executed. It's a grisly map. Disease as interpretation and anonymity. The plague itself as injection into certain subsets of opinion. Rich people. Plague sores, each basilica split open to various popular songs, calendars folded within them, recorded crackles through forcibly locked houses, through LEDs and meth. Basic surrealism. Aimé Césaire wrote years ago that 'poetic knowledge is born in the great silence of scientific knowledge'. And science itself the great silence at the centre of corporate knowledge, its dialectical warp and synaptic negation. As in a single node of extraction made up, for example, of the precise percentage of the world's population who will never again be called by name, except by cops and executioners. Each one of those names – and we know none of them – is the predominant running metaphor of the entire culture, a net of symptom splinters producing abdominal pain and difficulty breathing, which in turn leads to a sharp increase in arrest numbers throughout the more opaque boroughs of selected major cities. OK? Now write a 'poem'. Directly after the August Riots I went to one of the big public meetings, don't know why, guess I was feeling a bit confused. Or maybe just bored. The speakers were awful, patronising, professional, you know the type. But there was one woman who spoke, she had nothing to do with the organisation, they'd got her up there for obvious reasons, yeh, and she lived on an estate somewhere and her son had leapt 16 floors from a tower block window. He'd been on curfew and the cops had turned up, without warning, at his flat. To check up or something. Anyway, he leapt 16 floors down, and they told her he'd killed himself, 'and I know my boy', his mother said from top table, 'and he wouldn't have jumped, he wouldn't have killed himself, not for them, not for anyone, not for the cops', and her voice cracked a little and then she said 'and as for the riots, I thought they were fair enough, and I think there should be more of them, and more, and more', and then she stopped and there was some applause. Not much. She was off script. A few of us had our fists in the air, nonetheless. Anyway. Here's a statistic for you, a class metaphor, an elegant little metric foot: not one police officer in the UK has been convicted for a death in police custody since 1969. Get that? Thats how long I've been fucking alive. You get that? And I think that's what she was getting at, at the meeting: every cop, living or dead, is a walking plague-pit. And that includes the nice ones with their bicycles and nasty little apples. Like some kind of particle mould. They are all Simon Harwood. They are all Kevin Hutchinson-Foster. And are running, with crowbars and wheels, year by year, strata by strata, backwards into, well, what they used to call the deep abyss, or perhaps the metamorphosis of commodities. The unity of opposites, anti-constellations cutting through chronology, an injection of three droplets of the weather on Neptune into each malevolently flashing unit of time. Spectrums, butchers. 'Poetry', remember, 'is born in the great silence of scientific knowledge'. What do you think that means, 'the great silence'. I ask because I'm not quite sure. Hölderlin, in his 'Notes on Oedipus', talks about the moment of 'fate', which, he says, 'tragically removes us from our orbit of life, the very-mid point of inner life, to another world, tears us off into the eccentric orbit of the dead'. But he's not talking about 'fate' as in myth, or the number of fatalities taking place every year in police cells and occupied territories worldwide, or indeed the home of every benefit claimant in this town. He's talking about prosody, about the fault-line that runs through the centre of that prosody, and how that fault-line is where the 'poetic' will be found, if it's going to be found anywhere. The moment of interruption, a 'counter rhythmic interruption', he calls it, where the language folds and stumbles for a second, like a cardiac splinter or a tectonic shake. Again, a cracked metaphor, an abstraction or a counter-earth. Actually it's an entire cluster of metaphors, and each one of those metaphors twist in any number of directions, so that 'counter-rhythmic interruption' refers, at the same time, to a band of masked-up rioters ripping up Oxford St., and to the sudden interruption inflicted by a cop's baton, a police cell and the malevolent syntax of a judge's sentence. We live in these cracks, these fault-lines. Who was it, maybe Raoul Vanei-gem, who wrote something about how we are trapped between two worlds, one that we do not accept, and one that does not exist. It's exactly right. One way I've been thinking about it is this: the calendar, as map, has been split down the middle, into two chro-nologies, two orbits, and they are locked in an endless spinning antagonism, where the dead are what tend to come to life, and the living are, well you get the picture. Obviously, only one of these orbits is visible at any one time and, equally obviously, the oppo-site is also true. It's as if there were two parallel time tracks, or maybe not so much parallel as actually superimposed on each other. You've got one track, call it antagonistic time, revolutionary time, the time of the dead, whatever, and it's packed with unfin-ished events: the Paris Commune, Orgreave, the Mau Mau rebel-lion. There are any number of examples, counter-earths, clusters of ideas and energies and metaphors that refuse to die, but are alive precisely nowhere. And then there is standard time, norma-tive time, a chain of completed triumphs, a net of monuments, dead labour, capital. The TV schedules, basically. And when a sub-rhythmic jolt, call it anything, misalignment of the planets, radio-active catastrophe, even a particularly brutal piece of legislation, brings about a sudden alignment of revolutionary and normative time, meaning that all metaphors – like scurvy – come back to fucking life, creating a buckling in the basic grounding metaphor of the entire culture, wherein that metaphor, to again misuse Hölderlin, becomes a network of forces, places of intersection, places of divergence, moments when everything is up for grabs. Well, that's the theory. Riot, plague, any number of un-used potentialities we can't even begin to list. Christ, I can't take it. I've been awake for days. My hands are trembling. Plague. The opposite of solidarity. Or rather, solidarity itself: the solidarity of isolation and quarantine, of the bomb-zone or the ghetto. The great silence is full of noises. And that's what I mean when I talk about poetics. A map, a counter-map, actually, a chart of the spatio-temporal rhythm of the riot-form, its prosody and signal-frequency. A map that could show the paths *not* taken. And where to find them, those paths, those antidotes, those counter-plagues. Anyway, I hope that answers your question. It's a very partial account, for sure. There are hundreds of other points of access to the metaphor cluster engaged within the riot form: think about the Portland Rum Riots of 1855, for example. Or the Zoot Suit Riots of 1943. Their trajectories through the varying intensities of official and unofficial chronology, the music of the past re-emerging as a sheet of blazing gin flowing through Chingford. Like that time we marched on Parliament, burned it to the ground. Remember that? It was fantastic.

July 29th 2013 – September 8th, 2014

FROM HAPPINESS

It is impossible to fully grasp Rimbaud's work, and especially *Une Saison en Enfer*, if you have not studied through and understood the whole of Marx's *Capital*.

september 2003. we were wondering why the poets were silent
we: children's books, whisky, record shops
bombed orchards, paracetamol, refugees, circuit boards
the sun, god of fire
there we have a series of verbs. they pass to & fro as if no-one had
    seen them.
they go in and out of random houses. signal towers. border
    towns.
the course of study is that simple
the legality & opacity of poets
the noises scratched into them. real constellations: beggars,
    economy, detonation
december 2009. a review of the year
a hell for the hands, for the hair, for the mouth, for the law. an
    entire symphony
360 degrees. supernatural sobriety of discontinued nouns
the reservoir at dawn
direction multiplied by velocity. glimpses of improbable
    harmony

mayday. the alphabet was a system of blackmail
complacent, would skate on our regulated senses

'sister, I hear the thunder of new wings'
some crap about the immanence of vowels etc

(a) an offensively wholesome social milk
(e) understood fucking as a swarm of conformity. was
(i) what was locked there was. chatter, flies etc
(o) a stringent regime of structural reforms &
(u) well, targets, neutrality. a closed circuit of abstract numbers

& us, locked out. the alphabet was, ultimately, not ours
in any case, its mythological shells, its crumpled octaves &
spectra, zilch / the conversation a hierarchy of

eclipse (as in a universe, infinitely compressed)

our desires lack density & social flame

'our silence is powerful'
'the voices you strangle today'

early 2012. the latest news is
political flashes superimposed on our rooftops
it is thin, our cynicism, the latest distinct word
sometimes, when a specific distortion in the vowels is achieved
we can hear heaven. it is a kind of wall
all of our clear, musical nouns
the morality of our achievements, singing on the scaffold
& the riot squad have denied everything
our laws and our tastes, this is harmony
every possible combination of peoples and phantoms
our sobriety and victims, this is our alphabet
sometimes, we get sick of our pious barbarism
we leap screeching into hell
our immense, unquestionable affluence

I understood money as a knife, would
use that centrifuge > London, rotating
embers of an abstract city, capital
in red & black. It was sleeping, we were
awake inside it > the opposite is also true
has blocked the anti-matter of the speaking I
has secreted memory < confronted its being
as bourgeois love, that cannibal monstrosity
wherein government is at war with thought's
productions of transparency < a pretty little
enzyme dissolved our face's history, privatised
the place and the formula > consciousness
in exile, mass without number, insurrection
is value. Meanings excoriate the enemy language.

hell. we are pleased how your city
got bombed – it was like, sleeping etc
you dull young men / to spin gently &

with guns / these are our ecstatics
are control, in prison is cosmology
or to lick your finger / and burnt as

starlings / yes we love what your
speech was a bed we / are your lips
yours, we bargained for / we spoke

your nights of monstrous study / we
as in glycerine / as sexual research we
we shit in your fucking guts / hello

noon. we scraped the village clean
or as our philosophy suggested
it was an army, a screeching whirl

something as vague as / please, we
know by now what a sky is, like
an obvious cycle of yellowed light

& talk like that. your hands have
not taste of gasoline. a circle of
toxic birds. the sun, heavy with

not a chain of shredding crows
our circles / spires & phosphor
defeat without end. & safety in

tactic A: we are channelling public opinion's
central panoptic > each shop window > is
equal to a specific convulsion > a spectral
split where London can pay to view its past
its face < each face a specific idea / fixed, as
dictionary level A < here is fresh vowels, as
against 'them' > plated glass as widened split
the eighth ditch is Piccadilly < is that simple
bloc 1: wherein I have been saying / & ever
since we became their plated glass of public
shit > well I have been saying lies > like we
was the centre of London < I was yelling to
some cop > was an enemy ghost I thought
or trapped outside his circled limpid world

fire is physical time. is absolute unrest
or total war < interior logic of music's
new definitions. o friends > build bonfires

say we choked their mirror, a heated
flicker > or we know what people used
to eat in pictures < we are eating stones

newsflash. May 2010. what we liked were / vowel one –

was international nights of torrential study, was harmonic
our hydraulic calculations, your medicines, children's books

Nephograms! Votemeal! O magnetic puke
& bank stuff. These spheres piss us off, yeh,
like surface nukes. But still, our so clean hands
of lepers v. the lash / 360 degrees / servitude

or paraquat / the rust on your kill silver
just rose up in judgement? Shame. Insert
lamotrogine, my asphyxiant / howl, love,
with scatological equity, goldened charity

i.e. send flowers, fire, gems

vowel two, three, four etc / sorry, but was a discrete attack
& shyly encircled the disks of the law. or we can't find em

we hold ourselves safe on the roof of the world's love –
our phantasmagoric business plans, our study of the stars –

the islands of the dead –

from the English I inherit my love of alcohol, idiocy and violence –
but I do not share their closed borders, their bureaucratic exterior –

as our co-ordinates are magnetised, & as our exits have been
    seized
we have vanished, we heavy stones of destruction & light –

as our hands are not aristocratic, still less those of the market
we have come in utter sentiment, some small targeted acquies-
cence –

the angle is fearsome, the order of the day is wretched hope –

as your maps are out of commission, we visit you secretly
we circles of cancelled stars, we flying rags of brutal factory girls
would cover your face, would swallow in grace & molestation

George Osborne, god of love, we have spurned beauty

election day. terminal. a cluster of predecessors in the language
i.e. cells of racist light, in verbs, tumbling
Belgravia or something, an adverb
think of adjectives as refugees. you just shot em: here is a style
        guide –

(e) a deficit line –
(a) negates the interruption of the speaking I –
(u) a system of collective thought –
(i) unable / unwilling to find work –
(o) beyond a certain tenancy of stoic disdain –

I entered first. Target A was standing by the table
I hit him with the shield. Pinned Target to floor
I was foul and fair, would sleep in utter music

the bulletins, consist entirely of nerves
or harmony, pure infection of thought

we entered a respectful half-light, the names, we had achieved
glue and murder / or we were images, monuments, gospels

& in very obvious nitrates / from the English I inherit
my mean & bitter divisions, my very grievous hail –

mostly they have explained your world

they invented colours for the vowels –

(u) glyphs & harm. understood simply as in
(e) simply / public spheres or stones
(o) chemicals & stones
(i) feasts of hunger, simply as in, stones
(a) stones

'so anyway', while we were picking berries
pretty as a kidnap / 'our superiors'
o paradise. here is a small door.

- blue – the ultimatum expands on
- green – we presume the decision not
- red – magnetic idiocies, mostly
- white – our arseholes are different
- black – isolation in its pure phase

anxiously their faces, were not there
it was a kind of heaven, scraps of sky

cold wind. passengers and crew.

December 2010. a high metallic wire. content exceeds phrase.

slight shift in geometry / slight interruption
in the flow of their / crimson & guillotined
bacterial princes / shifted / rivets of history

ok. theirs is a more stupid alphabet. sections to be ringed and
taken away.
unspoken contradictions in their footsteps. a universe devoid of
images.
an october we thought we couldn't have. external symbols within
our sky.

back now to our studies. negation of the negation. we will raise
the dead.

4.30 a.m. the story of one of my idiocies –
this is all so far away –
two distant bangs & a high pitched noise –
the colours of the vowels –
would screech inside your calculations –
basic lies, vomit and alchemy –
the simple prison diagram –
18th October 1977 –
you were controlled circuits –
we were rusting inside your house –
o delight o music, the peace of calm lines –
o geometric faults, in denial & in anger –
my final recollection. hello –

it is not the cops > but geometry, from
this perspective is eerily silent about
its more scandalous projections < we
have scraped its clocks clean, we have
inserted a brown cigar, a cheap and easy
proto-tone, we have called it a village.
> oh hell. we are your population, turning
at 360 degrees, where King Charles I is
equal to or lesser than Ian Tomlinson, or
we already said that, forget it > we press
hands together, as scars of circling bone
where silence is also prohibited, funded
guns surround the city banks' networks
of compulsory metaphors speaking aloud

Lord Browne, from politeness
that particular thought is
an opportunity, a response
to that thievery, his silence –
he is though, representative
of certain constellations of order
obvious studies of number, and
the present apocalypse is
a structural problem, this
eschews metaphor, the enemy
'is', a defining molecule
he is though, a childfucker
a swarm of goldened thinking
dead behind the rose trees

                    *

----------------of Milton, Lenin
& Satan, of the scum of england,
of the years enclosed there, we
the cells of england, we smarted
inside these delicate circles, the
nettles of soviet england, of
isolation in its pure state, where
diamonds, insects, walk like tyrants

of Downing Street, that assembly of ghouls & defunct regimes
of the warm November wind, our absurd paupers' memories

outside London it is all geometry, a euphemism for civil war
I remember our cotton dresses, those ribbons and bows

we skirted the disks of the city, its deserted, dying angles

we were wearing flags and pretty flowers, but our memories
at several intersections they opened into vast arched domes

of that other life, its obnoxious circles, of relics and animal love
the horrific quantity of force we will need to continue even to live

*

When you meet a Tory on the street, cut his throat
It will bring out the best in you.
It is as simple as music or drunken speech.
There will be flashes of obsolete light.
You will notice the weather only when it starts to die.

--------------- here at the centre of the official world, they're making a chart of all of our secret thoughts. They know everything about our cities, our rented glue

(a) *the fusion of transnational capital with reactionary political power*
(e) *arbitrary militarisation*
(i) *a racist mobilisation against selected scapegoats*
(o) *public opinion's spectral ditch*
(u) *a fanatical ideology based on hypocrisy and sentiment*

It's all so exotic, a renewal of sectarian violence: like circus tyrants, they are bestial and tender / like sentimental magnets, they will occupy our territory for a single second, or maybe for months, maybe forever.

Trafalgar Square is solid meat. Dogs.

9th March 1871. a difference of opinion –

we were nouns, a black gulf where your speech is rusting politi-
cally –
an oracular diagram, moronic translations, music roasting –
a strange, distant english voice, bricked up inside it –

Hello, I'm the police. Like, you know, serious
like deliver your purse, or I'll / with your
red courtesans whirling, & our gross kettle
meaningless. We have no further comment

Howl, dole-rust, caustic half-dead city
scrape jet / surprise attack on human head
& its million doors / a gap obliterate
or oh I'm sober now. have rat will

but this is a very crude reading –
later we made art, it shattered nothing –
our homicidal lives now were a form of understanding –
our expressions were lifeless, our hatred made visible –

the point is an absolute redistribution of all the senses –

So I see you're a teacher again. November 10th was ridiculous, we were all caught unawares. And that 'we' is the same as the 'we' in these poems, as against 'them', and maybe against 'you', in that a rapid collectivising of subjectivity equally rapidly involves locked doors, barricades, self-definition through antagonism etc. If you weren't there, you just won't get it. But anyway, a few months later, or was it before, I can't remember anymore, I sat down to write an essay on Rimbaud. I'd been to a talk at Marx House and was amazed that people could still only talk through all the myths: Verlaine etc nasty-assed punk bitch etc gun running, colonialism, etc. Slightly less about that last one. As if there was nothing to say about what it was in Rimbaud's work – or in avant-garde poetry in general – that could be read as the subjective counterpart to the objective upheavals of any revolutionary moment. How could what we were experiencing, I asked myself, be delineated in such a way that we could recognise ourselves in it. The form would be monstrous. That's in *The Aesthetics of Resistance* somewhere. I mean, obviously a rant against the government, even delivered via a brick through the window, is not nearly enough. I started thinking the reason the student movement failed was down to the fucking slogans. They were awful. As feeble as poems. Yeh, I turned up and did readings in the student occupations and, frankly, I'd have been better off just drinking. It felt stupid to stand up, after someone had been doing a talk on what to do if you got nicked, or whatever, to stand up and read poetry. I can't kid myself otherwise. I can't delude myself that my poetry had somehow been 'tested' because they kinda liked it. Because, you know, after we achieved political understanding our hatred grew more intense, we began fighting, we were guided by a cold, homicidal repulsion, and very seldom did we find that sensation articulated in art, in literature. That was Peter Weiss again. I wondered could we, somehow, could we write a poem that (1) could identify the precise moment in the present conjuncture, (2) name the task specific to that moment, i.e. a poem that would enable us to name that decisive moment and (3) exert force inasmuch as we would have condensed and embodied the concrete analysis of the concrete situation. I'm not talking about the poem as magical thinking, not at all, but as analysis and clarity. I haven't seen anyone do that. But, still, it is impossible to fully grasp Rimbaud's work, and especially *Une Saison en Enfer*, if you have not studied through and understood the whole of Marx's *Capital*. And this is why no English speaking poet has ever understood Rimbaud. Poetry is stupid, but then again, stupidity is not the absence of intellectual ability but rather the scar of its mutilation. Rimbaud hammered out his poetic programme in May 1871, the week before the Paris Communards were slaughtered. He wanted to be there, he kept saying it. The 'long systematic derangement of the senses', the 'I is an other', he's talking about the destruction of bourgeois subjectivity, yeh? That's clear, yeh? That's his claim for the poetic imagination, that's his idea of what poetic labour is. Obviously you could read that as a simple recipe for personal excess, but only from the perspective of police reality. Like, I just took some speed, then smoked a joint and now I'm gonna have a pepsi, but that's not why I'm writing this and it's not what it's about. The 'systematic derangement of the senses' is the social senses, ok, and the 'I' becomes an 'other' as in the transformation of the individual into the collective when it all kicks off. It's only in the English-speaking world, where none of us know anything except how to kill, that you have to point simple shit like that out. In the enemy language it is necessary to lie. & seeing as language is probably the chief of the social senses, we have to derange that. But how do we get to that without turning into lame-assed conceptualists trying to get jiggy with their students. You know what, and who, I mean. For the vast majority of people, including the working class, the politicised workers and students are simply incomprehensible. Think about that when you're going on about rebarbative avant-garde language. Or this: simple anti-communication, borrowed today from Dadaism by the most reactionary champions of the established lies, is worthless in an era when the most urgent question is to create a new communication on all levels of practice, from the most simple to the most complex.

Or this: in the liberation struggles, these people who were once relegated to the realm of the imagination, victims of unspeakable terrors, but content to lose themselves in hallucinatory dreams, are thrown into disarray, re-form, and amid blood and tears give birth to very real and urgent issues. It's simple, social being determines content, content deranges form etc. Read Rimbaud's last poems. They're so intensely hallucinatory, so fragile, the sound of a mind at the end of its tether and in the process of falling apart, the sound of the return to capitalist business-as-usual after the intensity of insurrection, the sound of the collective I being pushed back into its individuality, the sound of being frozen to fucking death. Polar ice, it's all he talks about. OK, I know, that just drags us right back to the romanticism of failure, and the *poète maudit*, that kinda gross conformity. And in any case, it's hardly our conjuncture. We've never seized control of a city. But, I dunno, we can still understand poetic thought, in the way I, and I hope you, work at it, as something that moves counter-clockwise to bourgeois anti-communication. Like all of it. Everything it says. We can engage with ideas that have been erased from the official account. If it's incomprehensible, well, see above. Think of an era where not only is, say, revolution impossible, but even the thought of revolution. I'm thinking specifically of the west, of course. But remember, most poetry is mimetic of what some square thinks is incomprehensible, rather than an engagement with it. There the phrase went beyond the content, here the content goes beyond the phrase. I dunno, I'd like to write a poetry that could speed up a dialectical continuity in discontinuity & thus make visible whatever is forced into invisibility by police realism, where the lyric I – yeh, that thing – can be (1) an interrupter and (2) a collective, where direct speech and incomprehensibility are only possible as a synthesis that can bend ideas into and out of the limits of insurrectionism and illegalism. The obvious danger being that disappeared ideas will only turn up 'dead', or reanimated as zombies: the terrorist as a damaged utopian where all of the elements, including those eclipsed by bourgeois thought are still absolutely occupied by that same bourgeoisie. I know this doesn't have much to do with 'poetry', as far as that word is understood, but then again, neither do I, not in that way. Listen, don't think I'm shitting you. This is the situation. I ran out on 'normal life' around twenty years ago. Ever since then I've been shut up in this ridiculous city, keeping to myself, completely involved in my work. I've answered every enquiry with silence. I've kept my head down, as you have to do in a contra-legal position like mine. But now, surprise attack by a government of millionaires. Everything forced to the surface. I don't feel I'm myself anymore. I've fallen to pieces, I can hardly breathe. My body has become something else, has fled into its smallest dimensions, has scattered into zero. And yet, as soon as it got to that, it took a deep breath, it could suddenly do it, it had passed across, it could see its indeterminable function within the whole. Yeh? That wasn't Rimbaud, that was Brecht, but you get the idea. Like on the 24th November we were standing around, outside Charing Cross, just leaning against the wall etc, when out of nowhere around 300 teenagers ran past us, tearing up the Strand, all yelling 'WHOSE STREETS OUR STREETS'. Well it cracked us up. You'd be a pig not to answer.

ACKNOWLEDGEMENTS

Many thanks to the editors of the following publications, where some of these poems have previously appeared: *Hi Zero, Fiery Flying Roule, Cannibal Spices, The Internal Leg and Cutlery Review, Negativity and Negation, South Chicago Review, Past Simple, The American Reader, Veer Off, Armed Cell, Tengen Magazine, Vlak, Tripwire, The Other Room Anthology, Gaff, Folkebiblioteket, No Prizes, Revolution and Poetry, Dreamboat, Cambridge Literary Review, Sous les Pavés, Ny Poesi, Irish Left Review, Intercapillary Space, Poetry Salzburg Review, Axolotl, Damn the Caesars, Mute, Crisis Inquiry* as well as various flyers distributed at demonstrations and other disturbances.

Special thanks are due to the editors of Grasp Press (5 *After Rimbaud*), Crater Press (*For the Administration*), Openned (*The Commons*), Unkant (*Happiness: Poems After Rimbaud*), Punch Press (*Four Letters: Four Comments*) and Iodine Press (*Letters on Harmony*), for their encouragement and support.

Many of these poems, especially *The Commons*, and the first handful of *Letters*, contain a number of unattributed quotations. This is in the tradition of what in some areas of folk music is known as a 'cuckoo song', where the singer will intersperse their own lyrics alongside whatever fragments of other songs happen to come to mind, thus creating a tapestry or collage in which the 'lyric I' loses its privatised being, and instead becomes a collective, an oppositional collective, spreading backwards and forward through known and unknown time. These sources, just as in the old songs my work is inspired by, will remain anonymous. My ideal reader is one who would recognise some, if not most of them.

Likewise those to whom these poems are dedicated, with love and anger, will remain un-named. They are those whom, over the past years, I have struggled and fought alongside against those dogs of hell, those vampires of capital who continue to dictate the terms of our lives. They know who they are. These poems could not have been written without them.

Lightning Source UK Ltd.
Milton Keynes UK
UKHW020005110223
416836UK00014B/535